English Grammar for Speaking 1

Basic

Song Won

외국어를 빠르게 습득하기 위한 방법

어떻게 하면 단기간에 외국어를 유창하게 할 수 있을까요?
다중언어를 구사할 수 있을까요? 독학으로 할 수 있을까요?
빠른 길이라는 것이 있을까요? 혹은 어학연수를 가야 하나요?

제가 여러 가지 외국어를 독학하면서 몇 가지 깨달은 것들이 있습니다.
외국어를 공부하는 여러분들과 그 정보를 공유하기 위하여 이 글을 남깁니다.

우선 기본적으로 해당 언어에 대한 관심과 사랑이 중요합니다. 관심을 가지고 신경을 쓰는 만큼 많은 것들을 알고 싶어지게 되고 배울 수 있게 됩니다. 관심을 가지세요. 그리고 즐기세요. 언어를 여러 사람들과 즐기며 다양하고 새로운 경험을 할 수 있는 도구로 사용할 수도, 자신의 인생을 바꿀 수 있는 강력한 무기로 사용할 수도 있습니다.

외국어를 익히는 방법에 대해서 좀 더 자세히 알아보도록 할까요?

1. 문자를 외우세요.
문자를 외우지 않고도 말하고 듣는 것은 가능합니다. 음성을 듣고 기억할 수 있기 때문이죠.
그러나 독학을 하거나 글을 읽고 쓰기를 원한다면 문자를 외워야 합니다.

2. 문법을 공부하세요.
1인칭 대명사, 주격, 목적격, 관계대명사, 동명사 등의 용어나 성질을 공부하는 것은 오히려 방해가 됩니다. 언어학자가 되기 위한 분이 아니라면 품사의 이름과 성격들을 파악하지 마세요. 무엇이 주어이고 목적어이고 서술어이고 등을 알아내는 것을 공부하는 것이 아니라 어떻게 대입하여 활용하는지를 공부하세요. 단어의 원형들을 찾아내서 해당하는 문법에 대입해야 합니다. 예를 들어 한국어에서 '고 싶다'라는 문법을 공부한다면 가다, 먹다, 운동하다 와 같은 단어의 원형들과 '고 싶다'의 문법을 결합해 보세요. 단어의 원형에서 '다'를 제거하고 '고 싶다'를 붙여주면 문장이 완성됩니다. '가고 싶다, 먹고 싶다, 운동하고 싶다' 등과 같이 평서문, 질문문, 부정문('기 싫다')을 만들 수 있습니다. 간단하죠? 영어, 중국어, 일본어 등 그 외의 언어들도 마찬가지입니다. 가능한 한 단순하고 쉽게 이해하려고 노력해 보세요. 그 후에는 단어만 알고 있다면 본인이 원하는 문장들을 만들어 낼 수 있습니다. 한 가지의 문법으로 수 천 가지의 문장을 만들어 낼 수 있습니다.

3. 단어를 매일 조금씩 외우세요.

한 번에 10~20개의 단어를 외우는 것보다는 주변 사물들의 간단한 단어들부터 한 개씩 외워 나가는 것을 추천합니다. 주변 사물과 상황에 관심을 갖고 그 단어의 원형을 찾아서 늘 가지고 다니는 핸드폰, 메모장 등에 써 놓으세요. 그리고 자투리 시간(버스를 기다리는 시간, 지하철 안에서 있는 시간 등)을 활용하여 틈만 나면 그 단어를 봐 주세요.
포스트잇을 활용하여 본인의 동선에 따라 붙여 놓으셔도 좋습니다. (침대 옆, 냉장고, 전원 스위치, 책상 옆, 거울, 옷장 등)

4. 드라마나 영화로 공부하세요.

컴퓨터나 핸드폰에 본인이 공부하는 언어로 말하는 드라마나 영화를 다운받으세요. 그리고 그 언어의 자막과 함께 보세요. 먼저 드라마에서 배우가 대사를 말하기 전에 정지 버튼을 눌러 자막을 소리 내 읽어 보세요. 그런 다음 재생버튼을 눌러 배우가 말하는 것을 들으세요. 그리고 정지시키고 그 배우와 똑같은 말투로 흉내 내 보세요. 다시 그 문장의 처음으로 돌아가서 배우가 말하는 것과 똑같이 말해 보세요. 자연스럽게 될 때까지 몇 번을 계속해서 반복하세요. 이렇게 함으로써 그 배우의 말투와 억양을 익힐 수 있고 모르는 단어가 나온다면 검색을 하여 단어나 표현을 익히는 데에도 도움이 될 수 있습니다. 단순히 드라마나 영화를 자막 없이 시청하는 것도 도움이 안 되는 것은 아니지만 그건 좀 더 익숙해지고 잘하게 되었을 때 하세요.

5. 핸드폰, 컴퓨터 등을 이용하여 원어민들과 매일매일 이야기하세요.

펜팔 사이트, 어플리케이션, 전화, 화상 전화 등을 활용하여 관심사가 일치하는, 가능한 한 많은 원어민 친구들을 만드세요. 그리고 가능한 한 많이, 자주 대화하세요. 페이스북, 카카오톡 등이 단순히 친구의 안부를 주고받는 연락 수단 만으로만 쓰이는 것이 아니라 학습하는 언어에 노출되어 공부할 수 있는 환경을 만들어 주는 강력한 수단이 될 수 있습니다.

6. 원어민들과 만나고 어울리세요.

책상에서만 단어를 외우고 문법을 공부하는 것이 다가 아니에요. 공부하는 언어를 사용하는 원어민들을 만나세요. 그리고 그들과 어울리며 친구가 되어 많은 시간을 보내세요. 그 언어를 사용하는 환경에 최대한 노출되어야 합니다. 정말 절박하신가요? 그럼 원어민 룸메이트를 찾아 같이 생활해 보세요. 이제 막 공부를 시작했다고 창피해하지 마세요. 오히려 틀려도 뻔뻔하고 당당하게 말하세요. 그러나 본인이 틀린 말을 했다는 것은 자각해야 합니다. 한 번 실수를 하고 나서는 맞는 말을 생각해 보세요. 그러고 나서 맞는 말을 사용하세요.

7. 왜 그런지는 묻지 마세요. 맞는지 틀리는지를 물어보세요.

말을 하고 소통하고 싶으시다면 '왜요?'라는 질문은 하지 마세요.

가방이 왜 가방인지에 대한 이유를 알고 싶으신가요? 그럼 가방으로 불리게 된 역사를 공부하는 것이 맞겠지요. 공부한 외국어를 맞게 사용하고 있는지, 틀리게 사용하고 있는지는 궁금해하셔야 합니다. 원어민 친구에게 물어보세요. 한 명만으로는 부족합니다. 두세 명에게 다 같은 의견이지 물어보세요.

맞다면 계속 사용하세요. 틀리다면 고쳐서 사용하세요. 불규칙이요? 외우세요!

8. 그대로 받아들이세요.

처음 외국어를 공부하시면 모국어를 번역하여 사용하는 습관을 갖게 됩니다. 처음에는 조금씩 그런 식으로 접근하는 것이 빠릅니다. 하지만 시간이 지날수록 모국어로 번역하여 말하기는 좋은 습관이 아닙니다. 원어민이 책을 읽을 때 번역해 가면서 읽지는 않겠지요? 본인도 원어민이라고 생각하시고 그들과 같은 방법으로 읽고, 말하고 이해하려고 하세요. 처음엔 쉽지 않겠지만, 그것이 적응되면 머릿속에서 번역할 필요 없이 원어민과 똑같이 읽고 대화하는 것이 가능해질 것입니다. 들을 때 또한 마찬가지입니다. 들은 그대로 이해하려고 노력하세요. 적응되면 번역할 필요 없이 이해할 수 있습니다. 번역하는 습관을 버리고 그대로 받아들여 이해하세요.

9. 주변 환경을 전부 언어를 위한 공부의 수단으로 활용하세요.

예를 들어 밖에 있는 한 남자가 걷고 있고 한 여자는 전화를 하고 있으며 또 다른 사람은 운전을 하고 누군가는 커피를 마시고 있다고 가정해 봅시다. 그 상황을 그냥 지나치지 말고 공부하시는 외국어로 머릿속으로 생각해 보세요. "남자가 걷고 있어요, 그리고 여자는 친구와 전화를 하고 있어요, 그리고 흰 옷을 입고 있는 남자가 운전하는 중이에요".

옆 사람이 사람들과 대화하고 있는 것들도 모두 공부하고 있는 외국어로 생각해 보세요.

주변에서 일어나는 모든 일들이 언어공부의 수단이 될 수 있습니다. 언어를 공부하려고 유학 가지 않으셔도 됩니다.

10. 단순화시키세요.

어려운 단어를 사용하지 않아도 됩니다. 100% 일치하는 단어를 찾으려는 노력보다는 쉬운 단어를 사용하세요. 말을 잘하는 사람이란 각종 전문용어를 사용하여 설명하는 사람이 아니라 10세부터 100세까지 모든 사람들이 이해할 수 있도록 쉽고 정확하게 전달하는 사람이라는 것을 잊지 마세요.

외국어를 습득하기 위해서는 다양한 방법들이 있지만 사실 가장 빠르고 유용한 것은 모국어의 사용을 스스로 금지시켜 외국어만 사용하는 환경을 만드는 것이다. 그것은 바로 그들과 함께 생활하는 것이다. 모국어로 쓰이거나 들리는 모든 것을 외국어로 전환시키고 그들과 같이 살고 어울리면 많은 것들을 익힐 수 있다. 정말 잘하고 싶은 마음이 간절하다면 외국인이 자주 머무는 쉐어하우스, 게스트하우스 등에서 거주해 보거나 룸메이트를 찾는 것을 추천한다. 이 방법을 사용하면 유학가거나 해외에서 거주하는 것보다 더 효율적으로 외국어를 습득하는 것이 가능하다.

Unit

1   **알파벳 대문자 읽기 및 쓰기**

   A, B, C ...

2   **알파벳 소문자 읽기 및 쓰기**

   a, b, c ...

3   **알파벳 ph, th ...**

   ph, th, sh ...

4   **인사말**

   What have you been up to?

5   **숫자**

   one, two, three ...

6   **Time, Dates, Days**

   1 o'clock, 2 o'clock, 3 o'clock ...

7   **I am ___**

   (1) 저는 ___예요/이에요 ---------------------------------- 저는 학생이에요.

   (2) 저는 ___/요/어요/해요 ---------------------------------- 저는 착해요.

8   **Am I ___ ?**

   (1) 제가 ___예요/이에요? ---------------------------------- 제가 바보예요?

   (2) 제가 ___/요/어요/해요? ---------------------------------- 제가 착해요?

9   **I am not ___**

   (1) 저는 ___이/가 아니에요 ---------------------------------- 저는 학생이 아니에요.

   (2) 저는 ___지 않아요 ---------------------------------- 저는 착하지 않아요.

Unit

10 **I do ___**
저는 ___요/어요/해요 ------------------------------ 저는 가요.

11 **Do I ___?**
제가 ___요/어요/해요? ---------------------------- 제가 가요?

12 **I do not ___**
저는 안 ___요/어요/해요 = ___지 않아요
저는 안 가요 = 저는 가지 않아요

13 **to ___**
___에, ___러/으러, ___기 위해, ___에게/한테, ___까지

14 **in, on, at**
___에/에서

15 **I, my, me, mine**
저는, 저의, 저/저를, 저의 것

16 **Do ___**
___ 세요/으세요 -------------------------------------- 가세요.

Don't ___
___지 마세요 -------------------------------------- 가지 마세요.

17 **always, sometimes, often ...**
항상, 가끔, 자주 ...

18 **Let's ___**
___ㅂ시다/읍시다 ---------------------------------- 갑시다.(가자.)

Unit

Let's not ___
___지 맙시다 ---------------------------------- 가지 맙시다.(가지 말자.)

(please) Let me ___
제가 ___게 하세요 (해 주세요) ------------------- 제가 가게 해 주세요.

19   I was ___
(1) 저는 ___ 였어요/이었어요 -------------------- 저는 겁쟁이였어요.
(2) 저는 ___ ㅆ어요/었어요/했어요 --------------- 저는 착했어요.

20   Was I ___?
(1) 저는 ___ 였어요/이었어요? ------------------ 저는 겁쟁이였어요?
(2) ___ ㅆ어요/었어요/했어요? ------------------ 저는 착했어요?

21   I was not ___
(1) 저는 ___이/가 아니었어요 -------------------- 저는 겁쟁이가 아니었어요.
(2) 저는 ___지 않았어요 = 저는 안 ___ㅆ어요/었어요/했어요
저는 저는 착하지 않았어요 = 저는 안 착했어요

22   (1) I did ___
저는 ___ㅆ어요/었어요/했어요 ------------------- 저는 일했어요.

00   예외 단어 모음
'ed'를 사용하지 않는 예외 단어 모음

23   (2) I did 예외
저는 ___ㅆ어요/었어요/했어요 ------------------- 저는 잤어요.

24   Did I ___?
제가 ___ㅆ어요/었어요/했어요? ----------------- 저는 잤어요?

Unit

25 I did not ___

저는 안 ___ ㅆ어요/었어요/했어요 = ___지 않았어요

저는 안 갔어요 = 저는 가지 않았어요

26 for ___

___ 을/를 위해 -------------------------------- 당신을 위해

___ 동안 ---------------------------------- 1년 동안

27 I am ___ing

저는 ___ 고 있어요 -------------------------- 저는 울고 있어요.

28 Am I ___ing?

저는 ___ 고 있어요? -------------------------- 저는 울고 있어요?

29 I am not ___ing

저는 안 ___고 있어요 = ___지 않고 있어요

저는 안 울고 있어요 = 저는 울지 않고 있어요

30 I was ___ing

저는 ___ 고 있었어요 -------------------------- 저는 울고 있었어요.

31 Was I ___ing?

저는 ___ 고 있었어요? -------------------------- 저는 울고 있었어요?

32 I was not ___ing

저는 안 ___고 있었어요 = ___지 않고 있었어요

저는 안 울고 있었어요 = 저는 울지 않고 있었어요

Unit

33 I am going to ___
저는 ___ ㄹ 거예요/을 거예요 ---------------------------- 저는 갈 거예요.

34 Are you going to ___?
당신은 ___ ㄹ 거예요/을 거예요? ------------------------- 당신은 갈 거예요?

35 I am not going to ___
저는 안 ___ ㄹ 거예요/을 거예요 = ___지 않을 거예요

저는 안 갈 거예요 = 저는 가지 않을 거예요

36 I will ___
1) 제가 ___ ㄹ게요/을게요 -------------------------------- 제가 갈게요.
2) 꼭/분명히 ___ ㄹ 거예요/을 거예요 -------------------- 그녀는 반드시 올 거예요.

37 Will you ___?
1) ___ 줄래요/어 줄래요/해 줄래요? --------------------- 도와 줄래요?
2) ___ ㄹ래요/을래요? ----------------------------------- 그만할래요?

Will I/he/she/we/they/it ___?
3) ___ ㄹ까요/을까요? ---------------------------------- 그녀가 돌아올까요?

38 I will not ___
저는 절대 ___지 않을 거예요 ----------------------------- 저는 절대 포기하지 않을 거예요.

39 I can ___
저는 ___ ㄹ 수 있어요/을 수 있어요 ---------------------- 저는 할 수 있어요.

40 Can you ___?
1) 당신은 ___ ㄹ 수 있어요/을 수 있어요? ---------------- 할 수 있어요?

Unit

Can I ___?

2) 제가 ___ 도 돼요/어도 돼요/해도 돼요? ----------------- 제가 가도 돼요?

41 **I can not ___**

저는 못 ___요/어요/해요 = ___ ㄹ 수 없어요/을 수 없어요

저는 못 가요 = 저는 갈 수 없어요

42 **I want to ___**

저는 ___고 싶어요 -- 저는 가고 싶어요.

43 **Do you want to ___?**

(당신은) ___ 고 싶어요? ------------------------------------ (당신은) 가고 싶어요?

44 **I don't want to ___**

저는 ___고 싶지 않아요 ------------------------------------ 저는 가고 싶지 않아요.

= 저는 ___기 싫어요

45 **I want you to ___**

저는 당신이 ___기를 원해요 ------------------------------ 저는 당신이 가기를 원해요.

46 **Do you want me to ___?**

당신은 제가 ___기를 원해요? ------------------------------ (당신은) 제가 가기를 원하세요?

47 **I don't want you to ___**

저는 당신이 ___지 않기를 원해요 ------------------------ 저는 당신이 가지 않기를 원해요.

48 **I need to ___**

저는 ___ㄹ필요가 있어요/을 필요가 있어요 --------------- 제가 갈 필요가 있어요.

49 **Do I need to ___?**

제가 ___ㄹ필요가 있어요/을 필요가 있어요? ------------- 제가 갈 필요가 있어요?

Unit

50   I don't need to ___

저는 ___ㄹ필요가 없어요/을 필요가 없어요 ---------------- 제가 갈 필요가 없어요.

51   I have to ___

저는 ___야 해요/어야 해요/해야 해요 ---------------------- 저는 가야 해요.

52   Do I have to ___?

제가 ___야 해요/어야 해요/해야 해요? --------------------- 제가 가야 해요?

53   I don't have to ___

저는 ___지 않아도 돼요 = 안 ___도 돼요/어도 돼요/해도 돼요

저는 가지 않아도 돼요 = 안 가도 돼요

54   I should ___

저는 ___야만 해요/어야만 해요/해야만 해요 ---------------- 저는 가야만 해요.

55   Should I ___?

제가 ___야만 해요/어야만 해요/해야만 해요? -------------- 제가 가야만 해요?

56   I should not ___

___면/으면 안 돼요, ___해서는 안 돼요 ------------------- 제가 가면 안 돼요.

57   I must ___

(1) 저는 반드시 ___ 야/어야/해야 해요 --------------------- 저는 반드시 가야 해요.

You must be ___

(2) ___하시겠어요 -- 피곤하시겠어요.

He/She/It/They must be ___

(3) 분명 ___일 거예요 -------------------------------------- 그는 분명히 학생일 거예요.

Unit

58 (1) I have ___
  저는 ___해 봤어요, 저는 ___한 적이 있어요 ---------- 저는 가 봤어요.

59 (2) I have ___
  제가 다 ___했어요, ___해버렸어요 -------------------- 저는 다 끝냈어요.

60 (3) I have ___
  저는 ___해 왔어요 -------------------------------------- 저는 (10년 동안) 일해왔어요.

61 I have been ___ing
  저는 ___해 오고 있어요 -------------------------------- 저는 (가게를) 운영해 오고 있어요.

62 I would ___
  저라면 ___할 거예요 --------------------------------- (당신이 오면) 저는 행복할 거예요.
  저라면 ___하겠어요 ---------------------------------- (저라면) 포기하겠어요.

63 Would you ___?
  (1) ___해 주시겠어요? --------------------------------- 추천해 주시겠어요?

  (2) 당신이라면 ___하시겠어요? ------------------------ 당신이라면 포기하시겠어요?

  Would he/she/it/they/we ___?
  (3) 그 남자가 ___할까요? ------------------------------ (과연) 그 남자가 올까요?

64 I would not ___
  저라면 안 ___할 거예요 -------------------- 저라면 포기 안 할 거예요. = 포기하지 않을 거예요.
  저라면 안 ___하겠어요 -------------------- 저라면 포기 안 하겠어요. = 포기하지 않겠어요.

65 If ___
  (만약) ___면/으면 ------------------------------------- 피곤하면 쉬세요.

Unit

66 **When I ___**
　　저는 ___ㄹ 때/을 때 ------------------------------------ 저는 피곤할 때 커피를 마셔요.

67 **There is ___**
　　___이/가 있어요 ------------------------------------ (거기에는) 한 남자가 있어요.

　　There are ___
　　___들이 있어요 ------------------------------------ (거기에는) 남자들이 있어요.

68 **that, who, which**
　　___는 --- 자는 사람, 보는 사람 …

69 **자주 쓰는 문법 패턴**
　　It's easy to …, difficult to …

70 **자주 쓰는 표현**

P. 158 -- **Final Test 1**

P. 168 -- **Final Test 2**

P. 176 -- **정답**

영어의 특징

외국어를 학습하기에 앞서 그 언어의 특징에 대해 알아두면 조금 더 빠른 학습이 가능하다.

- 나, 너, 그, 그녀, 우리, 그들을 반드시 사용해야 한다.

- 문장의 첫 글자는 대문자를 사용한다.

- f, l, r, v, z, th 등의 발음은 한국어에 존재하지 않으므로 입모양과 혀의 위치를 파악하여 연습해야 한다.

- 줄임말이 존재하며 사용 빈도가 매우 높다. 예) want to - wanna

- 강조하여 표현할 때, 혹은 격식을 차릴 때는 줄이지 않고 원형을 그대로 사용한다.

- 존댓말이 따로 존재하지는 않지만 공손한 표현들과 격식을 차린 표현들이 있다.

- 영국, 미국, 캐나다, 호주 등 모두 영어를 사용하는 나라이지만 발음이나 억양, 자주 사용하는 단어가 다르다.

- 글로 영어를 쓸 때 모두 대문자를 사용하면 소리치듯 강조하는 뜻으로 사용된다.
  예) YOU DID WHAT?!

- 한 개인지, 두 개인지, 여러 개인지를 명확히 해야 한다.
  예) I have a book. I have two books. I have many books.

UNIT 01 알파벳 대문자

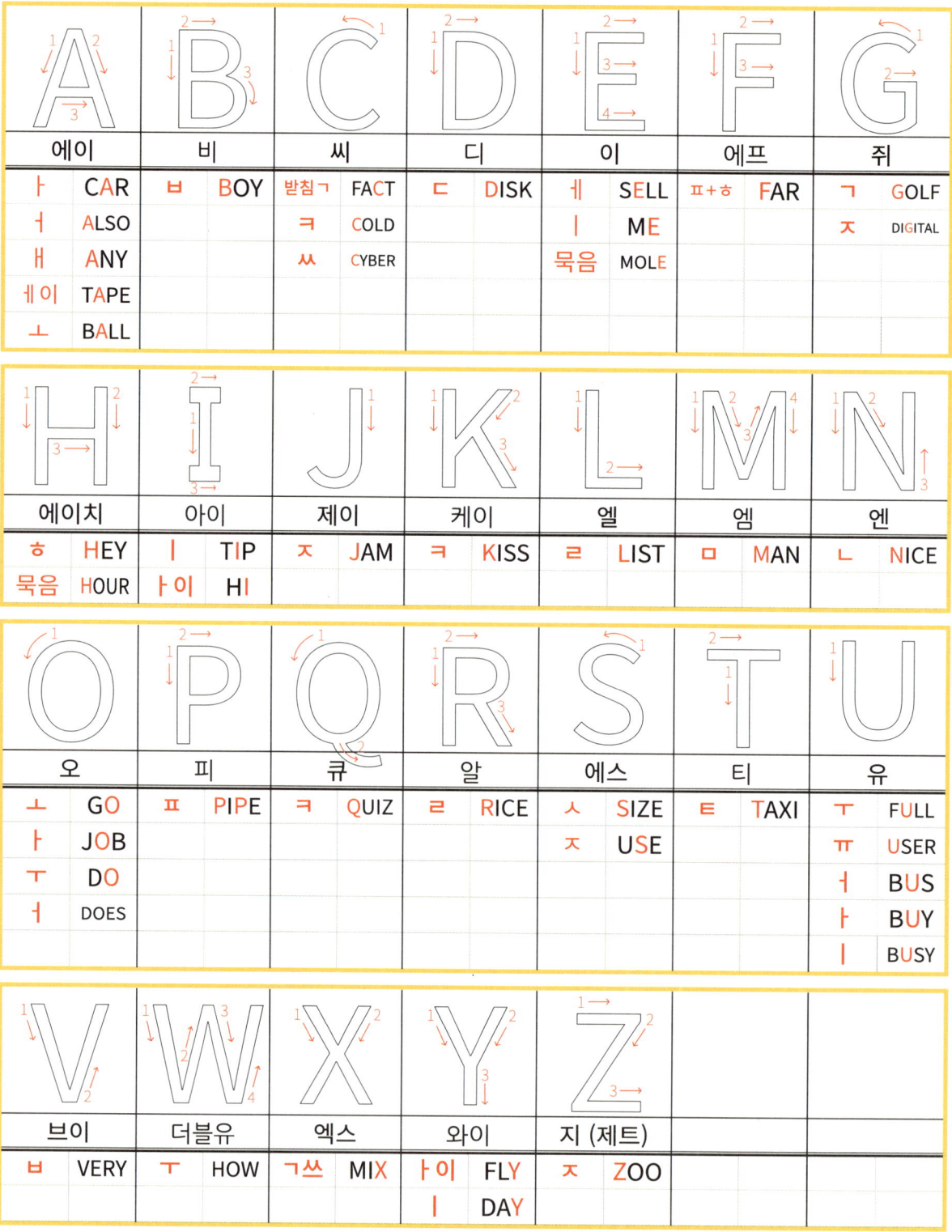

연습문제 — Unit 1

빈 칸을 따라 쓰고 읽으며 발음을 연습해 보세요.

CAR	ALSO	TAPE	BALL
BAR	COLD	CENT	CARD
DESK	SAND	PEN	FOR
GAS	GOLD	HELL	KID
LION	JAZZ	KOREA	LIST
MAGIC	NOW	POST	QUIZ
RISK	PASS	SAFE	TEST
TURN	CUT	HUG	VOICE
WILD	WEST	MIX	TYPE
HEY	GUY	ZERO	ZIPPER

UNIT 02 알파벳 소문자

a	b	c	d	e	f	g
에이	비	씨	디	이	에프	쥐
ㅏ art	ㅂ bed	받침ㄱ act	ㄷ sad	ㅔ pen	ㅍ+ㅎ fall	ㄱ gas
ㅓ dual		ㅋ card		ㅣ he		ㅈ gym
ㅐ ask		ㅆ ace		묶음 pole		
ㅔ이 face						
ㅗ all						

h	i	j	k	l	m	n
에이치	아이	제이	케이	엘	엠	엔
ㅎ hall	ㅣ pin	ㅈ jazz	ㅋ kick	ㄹ mall	ㅁ jam	ㄴ next
	ㅏ이 file					

o	p	q	r	s	t	u
오	피	큐	알	에스	티	유
ㅗ hole	ㅍ pig	ㅋ quit	ㄹ run	ㅅ slow	ㅌ text	ㅜ pull
ㅏ hot				ㅈ is		ㅠ use
ㅜ do						ㅓ us
ㅓ love						ㅏ guy
						ㅣ busy

v	w	x	y	z		
브이	더블유	엑스	와이	지 (제트)		
ㅂ van	ㅜ bow	ㄱ쓰 fax	ㅏ이 my	ㅈ lazy		
			ㅣ copy			

연습문제 Unit 2

빈 칸을 따라 쓰고 읽으며 발음을 연습해 보세요.

mask	ask	best	job
bike	cart	cat	back
date	do	egg	fan
fur	feel	surf	gift
mug	host	hot	kiss
pizza	just	dark	large
lips	miss	pan	nap
rose	stress	time	ugly
move	tow	west	pay
dozen	power	quit	lazy

UNIT 03 연음

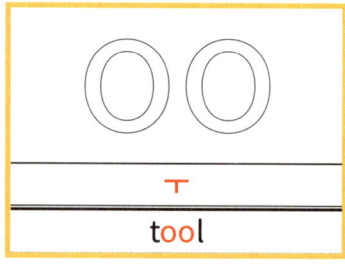

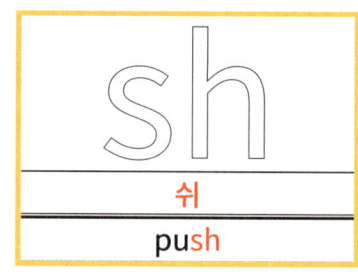
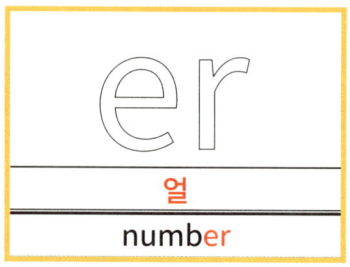
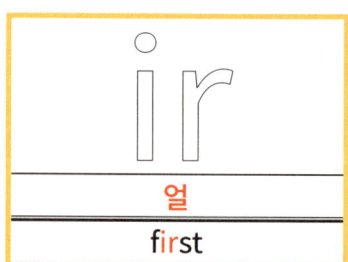
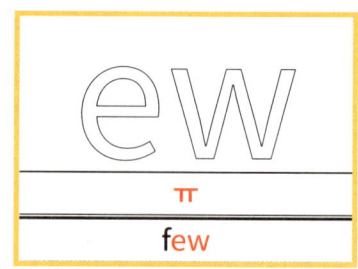

연습문제　　　Unit 3

빈 칸을 따라 쓰고 읽으며 발음을 연습해 보세요.

moon	fool	wood	zoo
bee	eel	feel	sheet
peace	easy	east	sea
phone	graph	photo	phrase
think	thank	nothing	thing
finish	push	dish	shoot
player	merge	permit	her
air	sir	girl	dirty
few	view	new	chew
sing	song	ring	lung
chick	choke	switch	touch
motion	fiction	mission	version

UNIT 04 — 인사말

Hi.
안녕하세요.

Hello?
여보세요?, 저기요?

Hey.
안녕, 야

Nice to meet you.
만나서 반갑습니다.

Good to see you.
만나서 반갑습니다.

Have a nice day.
좋은 하루 보내세요.

(I will) See you later.
나중에 또 만나요.

(I will) See you soon.
곧 봬요.

Have a good one.
좋은 시간 보내요.

Good bye.
안녕히 계세요/가세요.

Take care.
건강히 잘 지내세요.

Take it easy.
쉬엄쉬엄하세요.

How are you?
안녕하세요?, 잘 지내요?

How are you doing?
잘 지내고 있어요?

How's it going?
어떻게 돼 가요?, 잘 지내요?

Long time no see.
오래간만이에요.

It's been a long time.
오래간만이에요.

It's been a while.
오래간만이에요.

How have you been?
어떻게 지냈어요?

What have you been doing?
뭐 하고 지냈어요?

What have you been up to?
(지금까지) 뭐 하고 지냈어요?

What's up?
안녕? 잘지내? 무슨 일이야?

What are you up to?
뭐 해?

Not much.
별 일 없어요.

I appreciate it.
감사합니다.

Cheers.
고마워, 건배

I'm sorry.
죄송합니다.

I'm sorry?
뭐라고요?

You are welcome.
천만에요.

I apologize.
사과할게요.

No problem.
별 거 아니에요.

No worries.
괜찮아요.

Welcome.
환영합니다.

Congratulations.
축하해요.

Good job.
잘했어요.

Good luck.
행운을 빌어요.

Excuse me.
실례합니다.

Excuse me?
뭐라고요?

Well done.
잘했어요.

Be careful.
조심하세요.

연습문제　　　　　　　　　　　　　　　　　　Unit 4

1. 다음을 영어로 쓰시오.

1) _____ 오래간만이에요.
2) _____ 사과할게요.
3) _____ 잘했어요.
4) _____ 곧 봬요.
5) _____ 어떻게 지냈어요?
6) _____ 축하해요.
7) _____ 잘 돼 가요?
8) _____ 좋은 하루 보내세요.
9) _____ 괜찮아요.
10) _____ 실례합니다.
11) _____ 쉬엄쉬엄하세요.
12) _____ 뭐라고요?
13) _____ 뭐 해?
14) _____ 별 일 없어요.
15) _____ 조심하세요.

2. 주어진 문장에 어울리는 인사말을 고르시오.

1) Long time no see.　•　　　•　1) Not much. You?

2) What's up?　•　　　•　2) See you. Take it easy.

3) I appreciate it.　•　　　•　3) I'm doing well. How are you?

4) See you later.　•　　　•　4) No problem.

5) How's it going?　•　　　•　5) How have you been?

3. 주어진 문장에 어울리는 대화를 선택하시오.

1) Watch your language.　•　　　•　1) Excuse me?
　　말조심하세요.

2) What's going on?　•　　　•　2) Thanks a lot. You saved me.
　　무슨 일이에요?

3) I made it!　•　　　•　3) Cheers!
　　제가 해냈어요!

4) Watch out!　•　　　•　4) Nothing.
　　조심하세요!

5) Let's have a toast.　•　　　•　5) Congratulations!
　　건배합시다.

UNIT 05 Numbers
숫자

0	1	2	3	4	5	6	7	8	9	10
zero oh	one	two	three	four	five	six	seven	eight	nine	ten

11	12	13	14	15	16	17	18	19
eleven	twelve	thirteen	fourteen	fifteen	sixteen	seventeen	eighteen	nineteen

20	30	40	50	60	70	80	90	100
twenty	thirty	forty	fifty	sixty	seventy	eighty	ninety	a hundred

1,000	10,000	100,000	1,000,000	10,000,000
one thousand	ten thousand	a hundred thousand	a million	ten million

1st	2nd	3rd	4th	5th	6th	7th	8th	9th	10th...
first 첫 번째	second 두 번째	third 세 번째	fourth	fifth	sixth	seventh	eighth	ninth	tenth

* 위의 숫자를 보고 빈 칸을 채우시오.

0	1	2	3	4	5	6	7	8	9	10

11	12	13	14	15	16	17	18	19

20	30	40	50	60	70	80	90	100

1,000	10,000	100,000	1,000,000	10,000,000

1st	2nd	3rd	4th	5th	6th	7th	8th	9th	10th	11th...

연습문제　　　　　　　　　　　　　　　　　　　　　Unit 5

1. 주어진 숫자를 영어로 쓰시오.

1) 2 _____　　　2) 4 _____　　　3) 3 _____
4) 12 _____　　　5) 20 _____　　　6) 76 _____
7) 202 _____　　　8) 470 _____　　　9) 927 _____
10) 2,600 _____　　11) 7,350 _____　　12) 4,371 _____
13) 50,000 _____　　14) 78,000 _____　　15) 93,400 _____

2. 다음 질문에 알맞은 답을 영어로 쓰시오.

1) 오늘은 몇 년도입니까? _____
2) 당신은 몇 살입니까? _____
3) 당신의 핸드폰 번호는 무엇입니까? _____
4) 당신의 지갑에 얼마가 있습니까? _____
5) 지금 몇 시 몇 분입니까? _____

3. 가족이나 친구의 전화번호를 쓰시오.

1) _____
2) _____
3) _____

4. 주어진 단어를 사용하여 질문에 답하시오.

| floor 층　　th 번째　　century 세기　　week 주 |

1) 당신은 몇 층에서 삽니까? _____
2) 당신은 지금 몇 층에서 공부합니까? _____
3) 올해는 당신의 몇 번째 생일입니까? _____
4) 지금은 몇 세기입니까? _____
5) 오늘은 이번 달의 몇 째주입니까? _____

UNIT 06

Time, Dates, Days
시간, 날짜, 요일

Time

1시	2시	3시	4시	5시
1 o'clock	2 o'clock	3 o'clock	4 o'clock	5 o'clock
1분	**2분**	**3분**	**4분**	**5분**
1 minute	2 minutes	3 minutes	4 minutes	5 minutes

11 : 05	12 : 10	3 : 40	5 : 27	6 : 35
eleven O five	twelve ten	three forty	five twenty seven	six thirty five

아침	점심 (시간)	저녁	오전	오후	밤
morning	lunch (time)	evening	morning	afternoon	night

어제	오늘	내일	지난주	이번 주	다음 주	주말
yesterday	today	tomorrow	last week	this week	next week	weekend

Months

1월	2월	3월	4월	5월	6월
January	February	March	April	May	June
7월	**8월**	**9월**	**10월**	**11월**	**12월**
July	August	September	October	November	December

Dates

1일	2일	3일	4일	5일	6일	7일	8일	9일	10일
first	second	third	fourth	fifth	sixth	seventh	eighth	ninth	tenth
11일	**12일**	**13일**	**14일**	**15일**	**16일**	**17일**	**18일**	**19일**	**20일**
eleventh	twelfth	thirteenth	fourteenth	fifteenth	sixteenth	seventeenth	eighteenth	nineteenth	twentieth
21일	**22일**	**23일**	**24일**	**25일**	**26일**	**27일**	**28일**	**29일**	**30일**
twenty first	twenty second	twenty third	twenty fourth	twenty fifth	twenty sixth	twenty seventh	twenty eighth	twenty ninth	thirtieth

Days

월요일	화요일	수요일	목요일	금요일	토요일	일요일
Monday	Tuesday	Wednesday	Thursday	Friday	Saturday	Sunday

연습문제 Unit 6

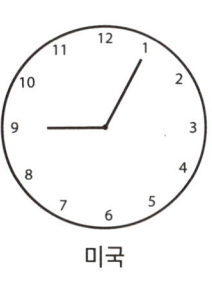
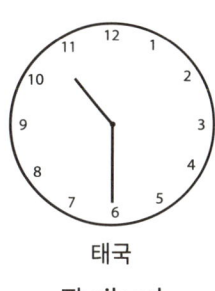

한국	중국	일본	미국	태국
Korea	China	Japan	America	Thailand

1. 주어진 질문에 답하시오.

1) What time is it in Korea?   It's 5 o'clock.

2) What time is it in China?

3) What time is it in Japan?

4) What time is it in America?

5) What time is it in Thailand?

2. 주어진 질문에 답하시오. *day: 요일, date: 날짜, month: 월, year: 년

1)
```
    2010 / 11
 1  2  3 (4) 5  6  7
 8  9 10 11 12 13 14
15 16 17 18 19 20 21
22 23 24 25 26 27 28
29 30
```

2)
```
    2017 / 7
           1  2  3  4
 5  6  7  8  9 10 11
12 (13) 14 15 16 17 18
19 20 21 22 23 24 25
26 27 28 29 30 31
```

3)
```
    2020 / 2
                    1
 2  3  4  5  6  7  8
 9 10 11 12 13 14 15
16 17 18 19 (20) 21 22
23 24 25 26 27 28
```

4)
```
    2025 / 5
          1  2  3  4  5
 6  7  8  9 10 11 12
13 14 15 16 17 18 19
20 21 22 23 24 25 26
27 28 29 30 (31)
```

1) What day is it today?

2) What date is it today?

3) What month is it?

4) What year is it?

3. 주어진 시간을 쓰시오.

1 : 05	2 : 20	3 : 45	4 : 17	5 : 30	6 : 09	7 : 41	8 : 50	9 : 12	10 : 10

11 : 00	12 : 03	8 : 14	7 : 28	1 : 18	4 : 46	5 : 33	3 : 52	6 : 07	2 : 22

UNIT 07

I am ___
(1) 저는 ___예요/이에요
(2) 저는 ___요/어요/해요

I ········· I am = I'm ·········

I	I am a student.	I am smart.
저	저는 학생이에요.	저는 똑똑해요.

you ········· you are = you're ·········

you	You are a teacher.	You are tall.
당신	당신은 선생님이에요.	당신은 키가 커요.

we ········· we are = we're ·········

we	We are co-workers.	We are awesome.
우리	우리는 동료예요.	우리는 대단해요.

they ········· they are = they're ·········

they	They are artists.	They are nice.
그들, 그것들	그들은 예술가들이에요.	그들은 착해요.

he ········· he is = he's ·········

he	He is an author.	He is rich.
그	그는 작가예요.	그는 부유해요.
	*a, e, i, o, u로 시작되는 단어는 an	

she ········· she is = she's ·········

she	She is a nurse.	She is adorable.
그녀	그녀는 간호사예요.	그녀는 사랑스러워요.

it ········· it is = it's ·········

it	It is a book.	It is unfair.
그것	그것은 책이에요.	그것은 불공평해요.

연습문제 Unit 7

1. am, are, is 를 알맞게 사용하여 빈 칸을 채우시오.

1) It ____ a bird. 새
2) He ____ a cook. 요리사
3) I ____ a receptionist. 접수 담당자
4) She ____ a designer. 디자이너
5) I ____ a model. 모델
6) They ____ actors. 배우
7) He ____ a gangster. 깡패
8) You ____ an artist. 예술가
9) She ____ an author. 작가
10) We ____ friends. 친구
11) It ____ a bicycle. 자전거
12) We ____ co-workers. 동료

2. am, are, is 를 알맞게 사용하여 빈 칸을 채우시오.

1) He ____ smart. 똑똑하다
2) She ____ tall. 키가 크다
3) He ____ cute. 귀엽다
4) We ____ stupid. 멍청하다
5) It ____ fair. 공평하다
6) You ____ nice. 착하다
7) He ____ sick. 아프다
8) It ____ unfair. 불공평하다
9) She ____ gorgeous. 아주 멋지다
10) They ____ adorable. 사랑스럽다
11) I ____ weak. 약하다
12) We ____ strong. 강하다

3. 알맞은 것을 골라 순서에 맞게 나열하여 문장을 완성하시오.

1) (am, I, a, cook)
2) (nice, she, is, a)
3) (he, rich, is, an)
4) (expensive, is, it, a)
5) (they, artists, a, an, artist, are)
6) (model, is, she, a) (a, gorgeous, is, she)
7) (a, teacher, he, is) (is, he, smart)
8) (actors, are, they) (cute, a, they, are)
9) (friends, friend, we, are) (we, are, a, tall)
10) (man, a, is, he) (nice, he, a, is)

4. 'am, are, is'를 사용하여 여러분이나 친구, 가족에 대해 쓰시오.

1)
2)
3)

UNIT 08

Am I ___?
(1) 제가 ___예요/이에요?
(2) 제가 ___요/어요/해요?

I — I am → am I?

Am I a robot?
제가 로봇인가요?
제가 로봇이냐고요?

Am I smart?
제가 똑똑한가요?
제가 똑똑하냐고요?

Who **am I**?
저는 누구인가요?
제가 누구냐고요?

you — you are → are you?

Are you a teacher?
당신은 선생님이에요?

Are you tall?
당신은 키가 커요.

Who **are you**?
(당신은) 누구세요?

we — we are → are we?

Are we co-workers?
우리는 동료예요?

Are we stupid?
우리는 멍청해요?

Where **are we**?
우리는 어디인가요?

they — they are → are they?

Are they artists?
그들은 예술가들이에요?

Are they nice?
그들은 착해요?

Where **are they**?
그들은 어디에 있어요?

he — he is → is he?

Is he an author?
그는 작가예요?

Is he rich?
그는 부유해요?

Where **is he**?
그는 어디에 있어요?

she — she is → is she?

Is she a nurse?
그녀는 간호사예요?

Is she cute?
그녀는 귀여워요?

Who **is she**?
그녀는 누구예요?

it — it is → is it?

Is it a book?
그것은 책이에요?

Is it unfair?
그것은 불공평해요?

What **is it**?
그건 뭐예요?

연습문제 — Unit 8

1. am, are, is 를 알맞게 사용하여 빈 칸을 채워 질문을 만드시오.

1) _____ you a student?
student: 학생

2) _____ he a professor?
professor: 교수

3) _____ she a manager?
manager: 관리자

4) _____ she a taxi driver?
taxi driver: 택시 운전사

5) _____ you a boss?
boss: 사장

6) _____ they co-workers?
co-workers: 동료들

7) _____ he a soldier?
soldier: 군인

8) _____ you an interpreter?
interpreter: 통역사

9) _____ she a teenager?
teenager: 십대

10) _____ they passengers?
passengers: 승객들

11) _____ it a book?
book: 책

12) _____ they photographers?
photographers: 사진가들

2. am, are, is 를 알맞게 사용하여 빈 칸을 채워 질문을 만드시오.

1) _____ we strong?
strong: 강하다

2) _____ it cheap?
cheap: 싸다

3) _____ they serious?
serious: 심각하다/진지하다

4) _____ it expensive?
expensive: 비싸다

5) _____ you crazy?
crazy: 미치다

6) _____ he old?
old: 늙다/낡다

7) _____ she young?
young: 젊다

8) _____ it rare?
rare: 드물다/희귀하다

9) _____ he alright?
alright: 괜찮다

10) _____ she okay?
okay: 괜찮다

11) _____ you hungry?
hungry: 배고프다

12) _____ it difficult?
difficult: 어렵다

3. 알맞은 것을 골라 순서에 맞게 나열하여 질문을 완성하시오.

1) (she, a, is, professor)
2) (you, are, a manager)
3) (a, it, expensive, is)
4) (serious, you, are, a)
5) (I, strong, am)
6) (Nick, a, student, is), (young, is, he)
7) (it, book, a, is), (it, is, difficult)
8) (passengers, are, they), (okay, they, are)
9) (Jessica, is, soldier, a), (is, she, strong)
10) (boss, a, is, Kevin), (rich, he, a, is)

4. 'am, are, is'를 사용하여 보기에 해당하는 질문을 만드시오. *when: 언제, how: 어떻게, why: 왜

1) 어디세요?
2) 누구세요?
3) 그건 뭐예요?
4) 그는 어디에 있어요?
5) 그게 언제예요?
6) 그게 왜요?
7) 그들은 어때요?
8) 그것들은 뭐예요?
9) 그녀는 누구예요?
10) 화장실이 어디예요?

UNIT 09

I am not ___
(1) 저는 ___이/가 아니에요
(2) 저는 ___지 않아요

I ─────────────── I am not = I'm not ───────────────

| I | I am not a part-timer. | I am not naive. |
| 저 | 저는 아르바이트생이 아니에요. | 저는 순진하지 않아요. |

you ─────────────── you are not = you're not ───────────────

| you | You are not a vegetarian. | You are not chubby. |
| 당신 | 당신은 채식주의자가 아니에요. | 당신은 통통하지 않아요. |

we ─────────────── we are not = we're not ───────────────

| we | We are not beggars. | We are not poor. |
| 우리 | 우리는 거지들이 아니에요. | 우리는 가난하지 않아요. |

they ─────────────── they are not = they're not ───────────────

| they | They are not prisoners. | They are not positive. |
| 그들, 그것들 | 그들은 죄수들이 아니에요. | 그들은 긍정적이지 않아요. |

he ─────────────── he is not = he's not ───────────────

| he | He is not a loser. | He is not negative. |
| 그 | 그는 실패자가 아니에요. | 그는 부정적이지 않아요. |

she ─────────────── she is not = she's not ───────────────

| she | She is not a teenager. | She is not weak. |
| 그녀 | 그녀는 십대가 아니에요. | 그녀는 약하지 않아요. |

it ─────────────── it is not = it's not ───────────────

| it | It is not a secret. | It is not awkward. |
| 그것 | 그것은 비밀이 아니에요. | 그것은 어색하지 않아요. |

연습문제 Unit 9

1. am, are, is와 not을 알맞게 사용하여 빈 칸을 채우시오.

1) A: Are you a teenager?   B: No, I am not a teenager.   I'm 35.
2) A: Is she a singer?   B: No,   She's an actress.
3) A: Is he a photographer?   B: No,   He's a pilot.
4) A: Are they birds?   B: No,   They're insects.
5) A: Is it a computer?   B: No,   It's a TV.

2. am, are, is와 not을 알맞게 사용하여 빈 칸을 채우시오.

1) A: Are you strong?   B: No, I am not strong.   I am weak.
2) A: Is it expensive?   B: No,   It is cheap.
3) A: Is he young?   B: No,   He is old.
4) A: Is she okay.   B: No,   She is sick.
5) A: Are you hungry?   B: No,   I am full.

3. 알맞은 것을 골라 순서에 맞게 나열하여 문장을 완성하시오.

1) (serious, is, he, a, not)
2) (am, not, I, rich, a)
3) (not, we, strangers, are)
4) (they, old, are, not)
5) (is, difficult, it, not)
6) (she, positive, not, is), (negative, is, she)
7) (is, it, fake, not), (is, real, it)
8) (teenager, I, not, am, a), (a, naive, not, I, am)
9) (they, vegetarians, are, not), (fat, not, they, are)
10) (weird, we, are, not), (normal, we, are)

4. am, are, is와 not을 사용하여 여러분이나 친구, 가족에 대해 쓰시오.

1)   4)
2)   5)
3)   6)

UNIT 10

I do ___
저는 ___요/어요/해요

I -------------------- do --------------------

I (do) study.
저는 공부해요.

I study English.
저는 영어를 공부해요.

you -------------------- do --------------------

You (do) work out.
당신은 운동해요.

You work out hard.
당신은 열심히 운동해요.

we -------------------- do --------------------

We (do) go.
우리는 가요.

We go to school.
우리는 학교에 가요.

they -------------------- do --------------------

They (do) drink.
그들은 마셔요.

They drink a lot.
그들은 많이 마셔요.

he -------------------- does --------------------

He (does) works.
그는 일해요.

He works in Korea.
그는 한국에서 일해요.

*he does work / he works 한 번 s가 나오면 그 뒤에 s가 다시 사용될 수 없다

she -------------------- does --------------------

She (does) likes it.
그녀는 그것을 좋아해요.

She likes coffee.
그녀는 커피를 좋아해요.

it -------------------- does --------------------

It (does) rains.
비가 내려요.

It rains often.
비가 자주 내려요.

NOTE

1. 괄호안에 do/does를 생략하지 않고 말하면 강조가 되며 뜻은 '네, ~해요!'로 사용할 수 있다.

2. he/she/it에서 한 번 s가 사용되면 (She likes it.) 그 뒤에 s가 다시 사용될 수 없다. (She does like it.)

3. 이 단어들은 s대신 es/ies를 사용한다. do - does, go - goes, study-studies, fly - flies

연습문제 — Unit 10

1. 'do'를 생략하고 주어진 문장을 영어로 번역하시오.

> work   remember   practice   eat   run   drive   work out   drink   move   go   learn

1) I study.
저는 공부해요.

2) He _____.
그는 일해요.

3) We _____.
우리는 연습해요.

4) She _____.
그녀는 배워요.

5) I _____.
저는 마셔요.

6) They _____.
그들은 먹어요.

7) He _____.
그는 기억해요.

8) You _____.
당신은 운동해요.

9) She _____.
그녀는 운전해요.

10) We _____.
우리는 가요.

11) It _____.
그것은 움직여요.

12) They _____.
그들은 달려요.

2. 'do'를 생략하고 주어진 문장을 영어로 번역하시오.

1) He drinks water.
그는 물을 마셔요.

2) _____.
그는 매일 운동해요.

3) _____.
우리는 당신을 기억해요.

4) _____.
그녀는 빨리 배워요.

5) _____.
저는 많이 먹어요.

6) _____.
저는 버스를 운전해요.

7) _____.
우리는 열심히 공부해요.

8) _____.
그녀는 커피를 좋아해요.

9) _____.
그들은 영어를 공부해요.

10) _____.
우리는 중국에 가요.

11) _____.
저는 한국에서 살아요.

12) _____.
그녀는 미국에서 살아요.

3. 주어진 단어로 문장을 완성하시오. *because: 왜냐하면, and: 그리고, so: 그래서

1) (I, Korean, study) because (in, I, live, Korea)
2) (study, English, I) and (I, every day, work out)
3) (eat, a lot, I) and (a lot, drink, I)
4) (we, China, to, go) because (China, in, work, we)
5) (like, coffee, I) so (drink, every day, I, coffee)

4. 알맞은 것을 골라 순서에 맞게 나열하여 문장을 완성하시오. *but: 하지만

1) (am, student, I, a), so (study, I, every day)
2) (remember, I, everything) because (smart, am, I)
3) (smart, is, she), so (fast, learns, learn, she)
4) (not, healthy, is, he) because (works out, he)
5) (study, I, Chinese), but (easy, it, not, is)

5. 1~10과에서 공부한 것을 사용하여 자기소개를 쓰시오.

UNIT 11

Do I ___?
제가 ___요/어요/해요?

I — — — — — — — — — — — I do → do I? — — — — — — — — — — —

I (do) know. → Do I know?   How do I know?
저는 알아요.   제가 아나요?   제가 어떻게 아나요?
    제가 아냐고요?   제가 어떻게 아냐고요?

you — — — — — — — — — — you do → do you? — — — — — — — — — —

You (do) work. → Do you work?   Where do you work?
당신은 일해요.   당신은 일해요?   당신은 어디에서 일해요?

we — — — — — — — — — — — we do → do we? — — — — — — — — — —

We (do) leave. → Do we leave?   When do we leave?
우리는 떠나요.   우리는 떠나요?   우리는 언제 떠나요?

they — — — — — — — — — — they do → do they? — — — — — — — — —

They (do) drink. → Do they drink?   What tea do they drink?
그들은 마셔요.   그들은 마셔요?   그들은 무슨 차를 마셔요?

he — — — — — — — — — — — he does → does he? — — — — — — — — —

He (does) complain**s**. → Does he complain?   Why does he complain?
그는 불평해요.   그는 불평해요?   그는 왜 불평해요?

she — — — — — — — — — — she does → does she? — — — — — — — — —

She (does) like**s** it. → Does she like it?   What kind of movies does she like?
그녀는 그것을 좋아해요.   그녀는 그것을 좋아해요?   그녀는 무슨 종류의 영화를 좋아해요?

it — — — — — — — — — — — it does → does It? — — — — — — — — —

It (does) rain**s**. → Does it rain?   How often does it rain?
비가 내려요.   비가 내려요?   얼마나 자주 비가 내려요?

연습문제 Unit 11

1. do와 does를 알맞게 사용하여 빈 칸을 채워 질문을 만드시오.

1) _____ you work?
   work: 일하다
2) _____ he work out?
   work out: 운동하다
3) _____ she drink?
   drink: 마시다
4) _____ she drive a truck?
   drive: 운전하다
5) _____ you speak English?
   speak: 말하다
6) _____ they live here?
   live: 살다
7) _____ you go to school?
   go: 가다
8) _____ you live in Singapore?
   live: 살다
9) _____ she like pizza?
   like: 좋아하다

2. do와 does를 사용하여 대답에 맞는 질문을 완성하시오.

1) A: _____ B: Yes. I work out every day.
2) A: _____ B: Yes. I live in England.
3) A: _____ B: Yes. I like cats and dogs.
4) A: _____ B: I go to school at 11 o'clock.
5) A: _____ B: Yes. She drinks green tea.

3. do와 does, 그리고 when, where, who, how, why 등을 사용하여 빈 칸을 채워 질문을 만드시오.

1) _____ you complain?
   왜 불평해요?
2) _____ he work out?
   그는 언제 운동해요?
3) _____ she drink?
   그녀는 뭐를 마셔요?
4) _____ I know?
   제가 어떻게 알아요?
5) _____ he like?
   그는 뭐를 좋아해요?
6) _____ they live?
   그들은 어디에서 살아요?
7) _____ you go to school?
   몇 시에 학교에 가요?
8) _____ you travel?
   얼마나 자주 여행해요?
9) _____ you like?
   당신은 무슨 영화를 좋아해요?

4. 순서에 맞게 나열하여 대답에 맞는 질문을 완성하시오.

1) (you, often, work out, how, do) A: _____ B: I work out every day.
2) (do, you, where, live) A: _____ B: I live in Seoul.
3) (what, like, do, you, animals, kind of) A: _____ B: I like cats and dogs.
4) (at, time, to, school, go, what, you, do) A: _____ B: I go to school at 3.
5) (take, how long, it, does) A: _____ B: It takes 5 hours.

5. do 혹은 does를 사용하여 질문과 대답으로 대화를 완성하시오.

1) A: _____ B: _____
2) A: _____ B: _____
3) A: _____ B: _____
4) A: _____ B: _____
5) A: _____ B: _____

UNIT 12

I do not ___
저는 안 ___요/어요/해요 = 저는 ___지 않아요

I — do not = don't

I (do) understand.
저는 이해해요.

I do not understand.
저는 이해가 안 돼요.

you — do not = don't

You (do) know.
당신은 알아요.

You do not know.
당신은 몰라요.

we — do not = don't

We (do) think so.
우리는 그렇게 생각해요.

We do not think so.
우리는그렇게 생각하지 않아요.

they — do not = don't

They (do) care.
그들은 신경 써요.

They do not care.
그들은 신경 쓰지 않아요.

he — does not = doesn't

He (does) regrets.
그는 후회해요.

He does not regret.
그는 후회하지 않아요.

she — does not = doesn't

She (does) follows rules.
그녀는 규칙을 따라요.

She does not follow rules.
그녀는 규칙을 따르지 않아요.

it — does not = doesn't

It (does) makes sense.
그것은 말이 돼요.

It does not make sense.
그것은 말이 안 돼요.

연습문제 Unit 12

1. don't를 사용하여 질문에 답하시오.

1) A: Do you work?   B: No, _____ because I'm rich.
2) A: Do you understand? B: No, _____ because I'm not a fast learner.
3) A: Does he care?   B: No, _____ because he is selfish.
4) A: Do you think so?   B: No, _____
5) A: Does it make sense? B: No, _____

2. don't를 사용하여 질문에 답하시오.

1) A: Do you drink wine?   B: No, _____ but I drink coffee.
2) A: Does she like it?   B: No, _____ because it is cheap.
3) A: Do you have a car?   B: No, _____ because I don't have money.
4) A: Does she live in England? B: No, _____ She lives in Australia.
5) A: Do they meet every day?   B: No, _____ because they are busy.

3. 알맞은 것을 골라 순서에 맞게 나열하여 질문을 완성하시오. *because를 사용하여 문장을 연결하시오.

1) (I, speak, English, don't), (Korea, live, I, in)
2) (she, have, doesn't, money), (she, work, doesn't)
3) (TV, doesn't, watch, he), (it, like, he, doesn't)
4) (hard, don't, work, they), (are, they, lazy)
5) (matter, it, doesn't), (happens, it, a lot)

4. don't를 사용하여 지인에 대해 쓰시오.

1) Nick doesn't live in Korea anymore. He lives in Canada.
2)
3)
4)
5)

UNIT 13

to ___
___러/으러, ___기 위해

에 — to

I go to school.
저는 학교에 가요.

She goes to church.
그녀는 교회에 가요.

I go ~~to~~ home.
*예외: home, here, there, inside, outside는 to를 사용하지 않는다.

러/으러 — to

I go to school to learn.
저는 배우러 학교에 가요.

She goes to England to work.
그녀는 일하러 영국에 가요.

기 위해 — to

We practice to win.
우리는 이기기 위해 연습해요.

I work to make money.
저는 돈을 벌기 위해 일해요.

에게, 한테 — to

It is important to me.
그것은 저에게 중요해요.

Please send it to her.
그것을 그녀에게 보내주세요.

까지 — to

It costs $20 to the airport.
공항까지 20달러의 비용이 듭니다.

It takes 30 minutes to the terminal.
터미널까지 30분이 걸립니다.

연습문제 — Unit 13

1. to를 사용하여 문장을 완성하시오. (에)

1) We go ___ school every day.   2) She comes ___ church.   3) He goes ___ the library.

4) I go ___ my friend's house.   5) They come ___ my office.   6) You go ___ the hospital.

7) He goes ___ the police station.   8) He comes ___ my place.   9) They go ___ the gas station.

2. to를 알맞게 사용하여 문장을 완성하시오. (하러)

| get a haircut   get some coffee   send a letter   watch a movie   work out   make money |

1) He goes to the gym ___   2) I go to the salon ___

3) She goes to work ___   4) We go to the cinema ___

5) We go to the post office ___   6) They go to the cafe ___

3. to를 알맞게 사용하여 문장을 완성하시오. (기 위해)

| travel to Peru   live   publish   sleep   sell   get a good job |

1) We study hard ___   2) I learn Spanish ___

3) They make products ___   4) I eat ___

5) She writes books ___   6) He lies down ___

4. to를 사용하여 문장을 완성하시오. (한테)

1) You are perfect ___ me.   2) It sounds good ___ me.   3) Don't do this ___ me.

4) Please come back ___ me.   5) I swear ___ God.   6) It means a lot ___ me.

7) She is really nice ___ him.   8) Talk ___ her.   9) Please give it ___ them.

5. to를 사용하여 문장을 완성하시오. (까지) *from: 에서,부터 by: 로/으로

1) How much does it cost from here ___ the airport?   3) It costs $100 ___ the airport by taxi.

4) How long does it take from Korea ___ China?   6) It takes 3 hours ___ China by airplane.

7) We work from 9 ___ 6.   9) She works from Monday ___ Friday.

UNIT 14

in, on, at
___에/에서

에/에서 — in

I am in a taxi.
저는 택시에 있어요.

I move to Hawaii in 2030.
저는 2030년에 하와이에 이사가요.

The bus leaves in 10 minutes.
그 버스는 10분내로 떠나요.

She lives in Korea.
그녀는 한국에서 살아요.

It starts in May.
그것은 5월에 시작해요.

It's cold in the winter.
겨울에 추워요.

위에 — on

I am on a boat.
저는 배 (위)에 있어요.

I work on Sundays.
저는 일요일에 일해요.

* I work this Sunday.
저는 이번 주 일요일에 일해요.

The books are on the desk.
책들이 책상 (위)에 있어요.

We ship it on May 20th.
우리는 5월 20일에 그것을 배송합니다.

에 — at

I am at home.
저는 집에 있어요.

I get up at 10 in the morning.
저는 아침 10시에 일어나요.

They are at the bus stop.
그들은 버스 정류장에 있어요.

I study at night.
저는 밤에 공부해요.

연습문제 — Unit 14

1. in을 사용하여 문장을 완성하시오.

1) He is ___ the hospital.   2) They work ___ Germany.   3) She is ___ the bathroom.

4) I was born ___ 1987.   5) I was born ___ August.   6) I have an exam ___ June.

7) I am ___ bed.   8) I live ___ Seoul.   9) The train leaves ___ 5 minutes.

2. on을 사용하여 문장을 완성하시오.

1) I have a plan ___ my birthday. 2) We work ___ weekends. 3) He comes ___ Tuesday.

4) A cup is ___ the desk.   5) A mosquito is ___ the wall. 6) There is a bug ___ the floor.

7) He has an exam ___ June 2.   8) I am ___ the subway.   9) There's something ___ your face.

3. at을 사용하여 문장을 완성하시오.

1) I wake up ___ 6 in the morning. 2) They go to bed ___ midnight. 3) We go out ___ night.

4) I work out ___ the gym.   5) We hang out ___ the mall.   6) I work ___ home.

7) They drink coffee ___ the cafe. 8) We study ___ the library.   9) I watch a movie ___ the cinema.

4. in, on, at을 알맞게 사용하여 문장을 완성하시오.

1) We are ___ the bus.   2) They are ___ a taxi.   3) She is ___ the plane.

4) I am ___ the subway.   5) It is ___ my bag.   6) He is ___ bed.

7) I am ___ the subway station. 8) We are ___ a car.   9) Your laptop is ___ the table.

10) I go to bed ___ 11.   11) They live ___ the city.   12) We meet ___ the weekend.

13) They are ___ Madrid.   14) Namsan Tower is ___ Seoul. 15) They are ___ the road.

UNIT 15

I, my, me, mine
(저는, 저의, 저/저를, 저의 것)

I ——————————— I, my, me, mine ———————————

I swear.
저는 맹세해요.

She is my girlfriend.
그녀는 저의 여자친구예요.

She likes me.
그녀는 저를 좋아해요.

This is mine.
이것은 제 것이에요.

you ——————————— you, your, you, yours ———————————

You remember.
당신은 기억해요.

Your bag is expensive.
당신의 가방은 비싸요.

He loves you.
그는 당신을 사랑해요.

This is yours.
이것은 당신의 것이에요.

we ——————————— we, our, us, ours ———————————

We promise.
우리는 약속해요.

He is our friend.
그는 우리의 친구예요.

She hates us.
그녀는 우리를 싫어해요.

It is ours.
그것은 우리의 것이에요.

they ——————————— they, their, them, theirs ———————————

They agree.
그들은 동의해요.

I use their tools.
저는 그들의 도구를 사용해요.

I use them.
저는 그것들을 사용해요.

These are theirs.
이것들은 그들의 것이에요.

he ——————————— he, his, him, his ———————————

He hesitates.
그는 망설여요.

I am his tutor.
저는 그의 과외 교사예요.

We trust him.
우리는 그를 신뢰해요.

That is his.
저것은 그의 것이에요.

she ——————————— she, her, her, hers ———————————

She knows.
그녀는 알아요.

He is her boyfriend.
그는 그녀의 남자친구예요.

I know her.
저는 그녀를 알아요.

Those are hers.
저것들은 그녀의 것이에요.

it ——————————— it, its, it, its ———————————

It moves.
그것은 움직여요.

I like its color.
저는 그것의 색을 좋아해요.

She knows it.
그녀는 그것을 알아요.

연습문제 — Unit 15

1. I, my, me, mine을 알맞게 사용하여 문장을 완성하시오.

1) It is _____ phone.
2) They are _____.
3) She doesn't know _____.
4) She respects _____.
5) Does he recognize _____? (알아보다)
6) I love _____ job.
7) This car is _____.
8) He is not _____ boyfriend.
9) Do you trust _____?

2. you, your, you, yours를 알맞게 사용하여 문장을 완성하시오.

1) Is this wallet _____?
2) I don't trust _____.
3) Is she _____ sister?
4) I owe _____.
5) Do I know _____?
6) These are not _____.
7) That camera is not _____.
8) Those are _____.
9) I don't doubt _____. (의심하다)

3. we, our, us, ours를 알맞게 사용하여 문장을 완성하시오.

1) His wife hates _____.
2) They don't believe _____.
3) Are _____ cool?
4) This house is _____.
5) He is _____ son.
6) _____ are not upset.
7) That's _____ story.
8) Those are not _____.
9) It's _____ dream.

4. they, their, them, theirs를 알맞게 사용하여 문장을 완성하시오.

1) _____ don't understand.
2) Tell _____.
3) It's _____ decision.
4) Don't ask _____.
5) I don't remember _____ names.
6) These are _____.
7) Those laptops are _____.
8) What language do _____ speak?
9) _____ like us.

5. he, his, him, his를 알맞게 사용하여 문장을 완성하시오.

1) I'm not _____ girlfriend.
2) _____ is upset.
3) Jenny loves _____.
4) This is for _____.
5) I don't judge _____.
6) It's _____ favorite.
7) I'm _____ brother.
8) _____ is my father.
9) It's _____ backpack.

6. she, her, her, hers를 알맞게 사용하여 문장을 완성하시오.

1) He doesn't recognize _____.
2) I don't take _____ lessons.
3) They doubt _____.
4) _____ doesn't know me.
5) _____ is not okay.
6) What color does _____ like?
7) _____ is Jane's roommate.
8) That purse is _____.
9) _____ sister is here.

UNIT 16

Do ___
___세요/으세요

be

Be a man.
남자가 되세요.

Be a hero.
영웅이 되세요.

Be a free man.
자유인이 되세요.

Be a gentleman.
신사가 되세요.

be

Be quiet.
조용하세요.

Be careful.
조심하세요.

Be confident.
자신감을 갖으세요.

Be gentle.
신사답게 행동하세요.

do

Go.
가세요.

Come.
오세요.

Wait.
기다리세요.

Move.
움직이세요.

---

please를 더하면 '해 주세요'

Please be my strength.
제 힘이 되어 주세요.

Please be patient.
참아 주세요.

Please support them.
그들을 지지해 주세요.

Don't ___
___지 마세요

be

Don't be a bad guy.
나쁜 남자가 되지 마세요.

Don't be a coward.
겁쟁이가 되지 마세요.

Don't be a fraud.
사기꾼이 되지 마세요.

Please don't be an idiot.
바보가 되지 말아 주세요.

be

Don't be afraid.
두려워하지 마세요.

Don't be silly.
어리석은 짓을 하지 마세요.

Don't be shy.
창피해하지 마세요.

Please don't be negative.
부정적으로 생각하지 말아 주세요.

do

Don't fight.
싸우지 마세요.

Don't push me.
저를 밀지 마세요.

Don't judge me.
저를 판단하지 마세요.

Please don't leave.
떠나지 말아 주세요.

연습문제 — Unit 16

1. 주어진 단어를 알맞게 사용하여 문장을 완성하시오.

> positive   follow   ask   keep   back off   have   confident   put down   trust   leave   listen up   pay attention

1) _____ me.
저를 신뢰하세요.

2) _____ him.
그에게 물어보세요.

3) _____, guys.
여러분, 잘 들으세요.

4) Be _____.
자신감을 갖으세요.

5) Just _____ it.
그냥 가지세요.

6) _____ me.
저를 따라오세요.

7) _____ a seat.
앉으세요.

8) _____.
주목하세요.

9) _____.
물러나세요.

10) _____ it _____.
그것을 내려놓으세요.

11) _____ me alone.
저를 홀로 내버려 두세요.

12) _____.
긍정적이 되세요.

2. 주어진 단어와 please를 알맞게 사용하여 문장을 완성하시오.

> put on   introduce   take off   promise   nice   recommend   come back   take   give

1) _____.
돌아와 주세요.

2) _____ the jacket.
그 자켓을 입어 주세요.

3) _____ your shoes.
당신의 신발을 벗어 주세요.

4) _____ me.
저에게 약속해 주세요.

5) _____ to her.
그녀에게 잘해 주세요.

6) _____ a picture.
사진을 찍어 주세요.

7) _____ her to me.
저한테 그녀를 소개해 주세요.

8) _____ a movie.
추천해 주세요.

9) _____ me a ride.
차를 태워 주세요.

3. don't를 알맞게 사용하여 문장을 완성하시오.

1) _____ ridiculous.
어처구니 없는 언행하지 마세요.

2) _____ jealous.
질투하지 마세요.

3) _____ late.
늦지 마세요.

4) _____ follow him.
그를 따라가지 마세요.

5) _____ touch me.
저를 만지지 마세요.

6) _____ listen to her.
그녀의 말을 듣지 마세요.

7) _____ worry about it.
그것에 대해서 걱정하지/신경쓰지 마세요.

8) _____ let me down.
저를 실망시키지 마세요.

9) _____ sad.
슬퍼하지 마세요.

10) _____ hesitate.
망설이지 마세요.

11) _____ ruin it.
그것을 망치지 마세요.

12) _____ rude.
무례하게 굴지 마세요.

4. 주어진 단어와 please don't를 알맞게 사용하여 문장을 완성하시오.

> negative   drive   leave   listen   ask   let down   ruin   touch   nice

1) _____ him.
그에게 물어보지 말아 주세요.

2) _____ me.
저를 떠나지 말아 주세요.

3) _____.
부정적으로 되지 말아 주세요.

4) _____ her.
그녀를 실망시키지 말아 주세요.

5) _____ to them.
그들의 말을 듣지 말아 주세요.

6) _____ it.
그것을 망치지 말아 주세요.

7) _____ anything.
아무것도 만지지 말아 주세요.

8) _____ too fast.
너무 빠르게 운전하지 말아 주세요.

9) _____ too _____.
그에게 너무 잘해주지 말아 주세요.

UNIT 17: always, sometimes, often
항상, 가끔, 자주

100% — always

I am always right.
저는 항상 옳아요.

I always work.
저는 항상 일해요.

90% — usually

She is usually kind.
그녀는 보통 친절해요.

She usually goes to bed at 10.
그녀는 보통 10시에 자러 가요.

70% — often

They are often selfish.
그들은 종종 이기적이에요.

They often make mistakes.
그들은 자주 실수를 해요.

50% — sometimes

You are sometimes stubborn.
당신은 가끔 고집을 부려요.

You sometimes smoke.
당신은 가끔 담배를 피워요.

0% — never

He is never nice to me.
그는 절대 저한테 착하게 굴지 않아요.

He never drinks.
그는 절대 마시지 않아요.

연습문제 — Unit 17

1. always를 알맞게 사용하여 문장을 완성하시오.

1) He _____
(things, buys, buy)

2) I _____
(work, hard)

3) They _____
(early, come)

4) ____ he _____ ?
(mistakes, make, makes)

5) ____ she _____ ?
(yells, yell, you, at)

6) ____ you _____ ?
(this, use)

7) He _____
(busy, busys)

8) She _____
(smiles, me, at, smile)

9) He _____
(late, lates)

2. usually를 알맞게 사용하여 문장을 완성하시오.

1) She _____
(coffee, in the morning, drinks)

2) I _____
(study, at the library)

3) They _____
(late, home, come, comes)

4) ____ you _____ ?
(at home, study)

5) ____ he _____ ?
(does, ask for a favor)

6) ____ it _____ ?
(snow, in September)

7) I _____
(study, studies, don't)

8) She _____
(work, home, from)

9) It _____
(snow, doesn't, in September)

3. often를 알맞게 사용하여 문장을 완성하시오.

1) He _____
(forget, forgets)

2) I _____
(skip breakfast)

3) People _____
(misunderstand)

4) I _____
(go out, goes out, at night)

5) You _____
(go there, goes there)

6) She _____
(change, changes, her mind)

7) My parents _____
(argue, argues)

8) Her son _____
(cry, cries)

9) James _____
(asks, ask, many questions)

4. sometimes를 알맞게 사용하여 문장을 완성하시오.

1) He _____
(annoying)

2) It _____
(useful)

3) It _____
(snow, snows)

4) I _____
(smoke, smokes)

5) You _____
(wrong, wrongs)

6) She _____
(weird, weirds)

7) They _____
(comes, come, here)

8) He _____
(watch, watches, TV)

9) It _____
(happen, happens)

5. never를 알맞게 사용하여 문장을 완성하시오.

1) He _____
(drink, drinks, alcohol)

2) I _____
(cook, cooks)

3) He _____
(reply, replies)

4) It _____
(enough, enoughs)

5) You _____
(checks, check, your email)

6) She _____
(understand, understands)

7) She _____
(right)

8) He _____
(listen, listens, to me)

9) I _____
(complain, complains)

UNIT 18

Let's ___
___ㅂ시다/읍시다

be - 되다

Let's be rebels.
반역자가 됩시다.

Let's be millionaires.
백만장자가 됩시다.

be - 지다

Let's be honest.
솔직해집시다.

Let's be serious.
진지해집시다.

do - 하다

Let's go.
갑시다.

Let's begin.
시작합시다.

Let's not ___
___지 맙시다

be - 되다

Let's not be enemies.
적이 되지 맙시다.

Let's not be troublemakers.
문제아가 되지 맙시다.

be - 지다

Let's not be rude.
무례해지지 맙시다.

Let's not be irresponsible.
무책임해지지 맙시다.

do - 하다

Let's not make noise.
떠들지 맙시다.

Let's not talk about it.
그것에 대해서 얘기하지 맙시다.

(please) Let me ___
제가 ___게 하세요 (해 주세요)

be

Let me in.
제가 들어가게 해 주세요.
(저를 들여보내 주세요.)

Let me out.
제가 나가게 해 주세요.
(저를 내보내 주세요.)

Let me be alone.
제가 혼자 있게 해 주세요.

be

Let him be angry.
그가 화를 내게 내버려 두세요.

Let me be frank.
제가 솔직하게 말할게요.

Let her be happy.
그녀가 행복하게 내버려 두세요.

do

Let me see.
제가 보게 해 주세요.

Let her go.
그녀가 가게 하세요.

Let me know.
저에게 알려 주세요.

연습문제　　　　　　　　　　　　　　　　　　　Unit 18

1. Let's를 알맞게 사용하여 빈 칸을 채우시오.

1) _____ take a look at this.　　2) _____ start over.　　3) _____ throw a party.
이것을 살펴봅시다.　　　　　　　　다시 시작합시다.　　　　　　파티를 엽시다.

4) _____ get over it.　　5) _____ honest.　　6) _____ roll.
그것을 극복합시다.　　　　　정직해집시다.　　　　　시작합시다.

7) _____ get started.　　8) _____ skip lunch.　　9) _____ go out tonight.
시작합시다.　　　　　　　　점심을 거릅시다.　　　　오늘 밤에 놉시다.

10) _____ have a toast.　　11) _____ check it out.　　12) _____ catch up soon.
건배합시다.　　　　　　　　그것을 확인해 봅시다.　　곧 만납시다.

2. Let's를 사용하여 작문하시오.

1) 　　　　　　　　　　2) 　　　　　　　　　　3)

4) 　　　　　　　　　　5) 　　　　　　　　　　6)

3. Let's not을 알맞게 사용하여 빈 칸을 채우시오.

1) _____ forget.　　2) _____ talk about it.　　3) _____ selfish.
잊지 맙시다.　　　　　그것에 대해서 얘기하지 맙시다.　이기적이지 맙시다.

4) _____ think too much.　　5) _____ get rid of it.　　6) _____ record this.
너무 많이 생각하지 맙시다.　　그것을 없애지 맙시다.　　이것을 녹화하지 맙시다.

7) _____ guess.　　8) _____ throw it away.　　9) _____ share this article.
추측하지 맙시다.　　　그것을 버리지 맙시다.　　이 기사를 공유하지 맙시다.

10) _____ waste resources.　　11) _____ rely on him.　　12) _____ exchange it.
자원을 낭비하지 맙시다.　　　　그에게 의존하지 맙시다.　　그것을 교환하지 맙시다.

4. Let's not을 사용하여 작문하시오.

1) 　　　　　　　　　　2) 　　　　　　　　　　3)

4) 　　　　　　　　　　5) 　　　　　　　　　　6)

5. Let someone을 알맞게 사용하여 빈 칸을 채우시오.

1) _____ help.　　2) _____ call you back.　　3) _____ show you.
제가 돕게 해 주세요.　　제가 다시 전화를 걸게 해 주세요.　제가 당신에게 보여주게 해 주세요.

4) _____ do this.　　5) _____ explain.　　6) _____ know.
제가 이것을 하게 해 주세요.　그녀가 설명하게 해 주세요.　그들이 알게 해 주세요.

7) _____ finish it.　　8) _____ stay here.　　9) _____ take care of it.
우리가 그것을 끝내게 해 주세요.　그가 여기에서 머물게 해 주세요.　제가 그것을 처리하게 해 주세요.

10) _____ guess.　　11) _____ tell you something.　　12) _____ pay for it.
제가 추측하게 해 주세요.　제가 당신에게 뭔가를 말하게 해 주세요.　제가 그것을 위해 (돈을) 내게 해 주세요.

6. Let someone을 사용하여 작문하시오.

1) 　　　　　　　　　　2) 　　　　　　　　　　3)

4) 　　　　　　　　　　5) 　　　　　　　　　　6)

UNIT 19

I was ___
(1) 저는 ___였어요/이었어요
(2) 저는 ___ㅆ어요/었어요/했어요

I ──────────── was ────────────

I was a designer.
저는 디자이너였어요.

I was young.
저는 젊었어요.

you ──────────── were ────────────

You were my hero.
당신은 저의 영웅이었어요.

You were short.
당신은 키가 작았어요.

we ──────────── were ────────────

We were friends.
우리는 친구였어요.

We were close.
우리는 가까웠어요. (친했어요)

they ──────────── were ────────────

They were foreigners.
그들은 외국인들이었어요.

They were kind.
그들은 친절했어요.

he ──────────── was ────────────

He was a firefighter.
그는 소방관이었어요.

He was poor.
그는 가난했어요.

she ──────────── was ────────────

She was a secretary.
그녀는 비서였어요.

She was cute.
그녀는 귀여웠어요.

it ──────────── was ────────────

It was an issue.
그것은 문제였어요.

It was tough.
그것은 힘들었어요.

연습문제　　　　　　　　　　　　　　Unit 19

1. was, were를 알맞게 사용하여 빈 칸을 채우시오.

1) You _____ a coward. 겁쟁이
2) He _____ a genius. 천재
3) I _____ an idiot. 바보
4) She _____ my girlfriend. 여자친구
5) I _____ a cleaner. 청소부
6) They _____ part-timers. 아르바이트생들
7) He _____ a businessman. 사업가
8) You _____ a magician. 마술사
9) She _____ a monk. 스님
10) We _____ waiters. 종업원들
11) It _____ a miracle. 기적
12) We _____ co-workers. 동료

2. was, were를 알맞게 사용하여 빈 칸을 채우시오.

1) He _____ nice. 착하다
2) She _____ awesome. 대단하다
3) I _____ young. 젊다
4) We _____ shy. 쑥스럽다
5) It _____ fantastic. 환상적이다
6) You _____ pretty. 예쁘다
7) It _____ exotic. 이국적이다
8) It _____ nice. 좋다
9) She _____ weird. 이상하다
10) They _____ amazing. 놀랍다
11) I _____ happy. 행복하다
12) We _____ close. 가깝다 (친하다)

3. 알맞은 것을 골라 순서에 맞게 나열하여 문장을 완성하시오.

1) (was, I, a, coward)
2) (I, was, a, businessman)
3) (my, ex-boyfriend, he, a, was)
4) (hero, she, was, a, my)
5) (were, you, a, awesome)
6) (they, weird, were)
7) (we, were, close)
8) (was, young, I), and (stupid, I, was)
9) (the concert, fantastic, was) and (it, worth, was, it)
10) (pretty, was, she), but (she, was, strange)

4. 'was, were'을 사용하여 본인이나 친구, 가족에 대해 쓰시오.

1)
2)
3)
4)
5)
6)

UNIT 20

Was I ___?
(1) 제가 ___였어요/이었어요?
(2) 제가 ___ㅆ어요/었어요/했어요?

I
I was → was I?

Was I a good husband?
제가 좋은 남편이었냐고요?
저는 좋은 남편이었나요?

Was I unhappy?
제가 불행했었냐고요?
제가 불행했었나요?

Where **was I**?
제가 어디에 있었냐고요?

you
you were → were you?

Were you an athlete?
당신은 운동선수였어요?

Were you strong?
당신은 힘이 셌어요?

Where **were you**?
어디에 있었어요?

we
we were → were we?

Were we troublemakers?
우리는 문제아들이었어요?

Were we weak?
우리는 (힘이) 약했어요?

Where **were we**?
우리는 어디에 있었어요?
(우리가 어디에 있었더라?)

they
they were → were they?

Were they criminals?
그들은 범죄자들이었어요?

Were they nice?
그들은 착했어요?

Who **were they**?
그들은 누구였어요?

he
he was → was he?

Was he a celebrity?
그는 연예인이었어요?

Was he poor?
그는 가난했어요?

Where **was he**?
그는 어디에 있었어요?

she
she was → was she?

Was she a painter?
그녀는 화가였어요?

Was she adorable?
그녀는 사랑스러웠어요?

Who **was she**?
그녀는 누구였어요?

it
it was → was it?

Was it a cup?
그것은 컵이었어요?

Was it awesome?
그것은 굉장했어요?

How **was it**?
(그것은) 어땠어요?

연습문제 Unit 20

1. was, were를 알맞게 사용하여 빈 칸을 채워 질문을 만드시오.

1) _____ you a security guard? 보안 요원
2) _____ she a secretary? 비서
3) _____ he a cook? 요리사
4) _____ he an actor? 배우
5) _____ you a comedian? 코미디언
6) _____ they developers? 개발자들
7) _____ she a celebrity? 연예인
8) _____ you a poet? 시인
9) _____ she a customer? 손님
10) _____ they adults? 어른들
11) _____ it a picture? 그림, 사진
12) _____ we instructors? 강사들

2. was, were를 사용하여 대답에 맞는 질문을 완성하시오.

1) A: _____ B: Yes, I was a comedian.
2) A: _____ B: Yes, she was a celebrity.
3) A: _____ B: Yes, he was a security guard.
4) A: _____ B: Yes, it was a picture.
5) A: _____ B: Yes, they were actors.

3. was, were를 알맞게 사용하여 빈 칸을 채워 질문을 만드시오.

1) _____ it different? 다르다
2) _____ it big? 크다
3) _____ they cute? 귀엽다
4) _____ she short? 키가 작다
5) _____ you lonely? 외롭다
6) _____ he nice? 착하다
7) _____ he sick? 아프다
8) _____ It different? 다르다
9) _____ it difficult? 어렵다
10) _____ it easy? 쉽다
11) _____ you happy? 행복하다
12) _____ she beautiful? 아름답다

4. was, were를 사용하여 대답에 맞는 질문을 완성하시오.

1) A: _____ B: Yes, It was awesome.
2) A: _____ B: Yes, he was cute.
3) A: _____ B: Yes, she was adorable.
4) A: _____ B: Yes, it was okay.
5) A: _____ B: Yes, they were amazing.

5. was, were를 사용하여 주어진 문장을 번역하시오.

1) (그것은) 어땠어요? _____
2) (그것들은) 어디에 있었어요? _____
3) (당신은) 왜 그곳에 있었어요? _____
4) (그것은) 뭐였어요?/뭐였더라 _____
5) (그것은) 언제였어요?/언제였더라 _____
6) (그것은) 누구였어요?/누구였더라 _____

UNIT 21

I was not ___
(1) 저는 ___이/가 아니었어요
(2) ___지 않았다 = 안___ㅆ어요/었어요/했어요

I — I was not → I wasn't

I was not a leader.
저는 지도자가 아니었어요.

I was not confident.
저는 자신이 없었어요.

you — you were not → you weren't

You were not a liar.
당신은 거짓말쟁이가 아니었어요.

You were not fat.
당신은 뚱뚱하지 않았어요.

we — we were not → we weren't

We were not co-workers.
우리는 직장동료가 아니었어요.

We were not selfish.
우리는 이기적이지 않았어요.

they — they were not → they weren't

They were not criminals.
그들은 범죄자들이 아니었어요.

They were not terrible.
그들은 안 끔찍했어요.

he — he was not → he wasn't

He was not a plumber.
그는 배관공이 아니었어요.

He was not rich.
그는 부유하지 않았어요.

she — she was not → she wasn't

She was not an employee.
그녀는 직원이 아니었어요.

She was not honest.
그녀는 정직하지 않았어요.

it — it was not → it wasn't

It was not a secret.
그것은 비밀이 아니었어요.

It was not expensive.
그것은 안 비쌌어요.

연습문제　　　　　　　　　　　　　　Unit 21

1. was, were과 not을 알맞게 사용하여 빈 칸을 채우시오.

1) You _____ alone. 　　2) He _____ a winner. 　　3) I _____ a loser.
　　　혼자　　　　　　　　　　　　　　승자　　　　　　　　　　　　　　패자

4) She _____ a liar. 　　5) It _____ $200. 　　6) They _____ animals.
　　　거짓말쟁이　　　　　　　　　200달러　　　　　　　　　　　　동물

7) He _____ positive. 　　8) You _____ negative. 　　9) She _____ selfish.
　　　긍정적이다　　　　　　　　　부정적이다　　　　　　　　　　　이기적이다

10) We _____ polite. 　　11) It _____ a coincidence. 　12) We _____ upset.
　　　정중하다　　　　　　　　　　우연　　　　　　　　　　　　　　화나다

2. was, were과 not을 알맞게 사용하여 빈 칸을 채우시오.

1) A: Were you a businessman?　　B: No, I wasn't a businessman. I was a lawyer.

2) A: Was she a dancer?　　　　　B: No, _____ She was a singer.

3) A: Was he a designer?　　　　　B: No, _____ He was a hairdresser.

4) A: Were they husband and wife? B: No, _____ They were friends.

5) A: Was it a ghost?　　　　　　 B: No, _____ It was a person.

3. was, were과 not을 알맞게 사용하여 빈 칸을 채우시오.

1) A: Were you tall?　　　B: No, _____ I was short.

2) A: Was it pricey?　　　B: No, _____ It was very cheap.

3) A: Was he loud?　　　　B: No, _____ He was quiet.

4) A: Was she cool?　　　 B: No, _____ She was picky.

5) A: Were you upset?　　 B: No, _____ I was tired.

4. was not을 사용하여 본인이나 친구, 가족에 대해 쓰시오.

1)

2)

3)

4)

5)

UNIT 22 (1) I Did ___
저는 ___ㅆ어요/었어요/했어요

I ——————————————— ed ———————————————

work	I did work. →	I worked.	I worked today.
일하다	네, 저는 일했어요.	저는 일했어요.	저는 오늘 일했어요.

you ——————————————— ed ———————————————

travel	You did travel. →	You traveled.	You traveled the world.
여행하다	네, 당신은 여행했어요.	당신은 여행했어요.	당신은 세상을 여행했어요.

we ——————————————— ed ———————————————

talk	We did talk. →	We talked.	We talked a lot.
얘기하다	네, 우리는 얘기했어요.	우리는 얘기했어요.	우리는 많이 얘기했어요.

they ——————————————— ed ———————————————

walk	They did walk. →	They walked.	They walked 10 kilometers.
걷다	네, 그들은 걸었어요.	그들은 걸었어요.	그들은 10킬로미터를 걸었어요.

he ——————————————— ed ———————————————

stay	He did stay. →	He stayed.	He stayed in a hotel.
머무르다	네, 그는 머물렀어요.	그는 머물렀어요.	그는 호텔에서 머물렀어요.

she ——————————————— ed ———————————————

watch	She did watch. →	She watched.	She watched TV.
보다	네, 그녀는 봤어요.	그녀는 봤어요.	그녀는 티비를 봤어요.

it ——————————————— ed ———————————————

snow	It did snow. →	It snowed.	It snowed a lot.
눈이 내리다	네, 눈이 내렸어요.	눈이 내렸어요.	눈이 많이 내렸어요.

NOTE

1. ed를 사용하지 않고 did를 사용하여 말하면 강조가 되며 뜻은 '네, ~해요!'로 사용할 수 있다.
2. y로 끝나는 단어는 ied를 사용한다. try - tried, study - studied 예외)play, enjoy, stay 등

연습문제 Unit 22

1. 'ed'를 사용하여 주어진 문장을 영어로 번역하시오.

1) I _____ .
저는 많이 배웠어요.

2) He _____ all around the world.
그는 전 세계를 여행했어요.

3) We _____ all day long.
우리는 하루 종일 얘기했어요.

4) She _____ it.
그녀는 그것을 사용했어요.

5) I _____ TV.
저는 티비를 봤어요.

6) They _____ a lot.
그들은 많이 연습했어요.

7) He _____ her.
그는 그녀를 사랑했어요.

8) She _____ him.
그녀는 그를 싫어했어요.

9) I _____ you.
저는 당신을 좋아했어요.

10) I _____ in Australia.
저는 호주에서 살았어요.

11) It _____ every day.
매일 비가 내렸어요.

12) They _____ for us.
그들은 우리들을 위해서 기다렸어요.

2. 주어진 단어를 사용하여 다음을 번역하시오.

> pack   play   fix   work   finish   call   cook   return   text   drop   download   cry

1) I _____ .
저는 그것을 다운받았어요.

2) _____ .
그가 그것을 떨어트렸어요.

3) _____ .
우리는 골프를 쳤어요.

4) _____ .
제 친구가 요리했어요.

5) _____ .
저는 하루 종일 일했어요.

6) _____ .
저는 울었어요.

7) _____ .
우리는 어제 그것을 반납했어요.

8) _____ .
그가 어젯밤에 저에게 전화했어요.

9) _____ .
우리는 짐을 다 쌌어요.

10) _____ .
저는 지난 주말에 그녀에게 문자를 했어요.

11) _____ .
그녀가 모든 것을 고쳤어요.

12) _____ .
저는 제 숙제를 끝냈어요.

3. 주어진 문장에서 밑줄 친 부분에 'ed'를 사용하여 '~했어요'로 문장을 완성하시오.

1) I play tennis because I like to exercise.

2) He pronounce it wrong.

3) I borrow this book from a friend of mine.

4) I charge my phone at a convenience store.

5) They help me a lot.

4. 주어진 단어에 'ed'를 사용하여 '~했어요'로 문장을 만드시오.

1) (print)

2) (install)

3) (sign up)

4) (enjoy)

5) (search)

5. 'ed'를 사용하여 오늘 일어난 모든 일들을 쓰시오.

'ed'를 사용하지 않는 예외 단어 모음

①	②	③	①	②	③
see 보다	saw 봤다	seen 봤었다	have 있다, 가지다	had 있었다, 가졌다	had 가졌었다
eat 먹다	ate 먹었다	eaten 먹었었다	take 가지고 가다	took 가지고 갔다	taken 가지고 갔었다
drink 마시다	drank 마셨다	drunk 마셨었다	come 오다	came 왔다	come 왔었다
go 가다	went 갔다	gone 갔었다	lose 잃어버리다	lost 잃어버렸다	lost 잃어버렸었다
sleep 자다	slept 잤다	slept 잤었다	sit 앉다	sat 앉았다	sat 앉았었다
wear 입다	wore 입었다	worn 입었었다	bring 가지고 오다	brought 가지고 왔다	brought 가지고 왔었다
buy 사다	bought 샀다	bought 샀었다	find 찾다	found 찾았다	found 찾았었다
sell 팔다	sold 팔았다	sold 팔았었다	do 하다	did 했다	done 했었다
choose 선택하다	chose 선택했다	chosen 선택했었다	catch 잡다	caught 잡았다	caught 잡았었다
send 보내다	sent 보냈다	sent 보냈었다	fight 싸우다	fought 싸웠다	fought 싸웠었다
write 쓰다	wrote 썼다	written 썼었다	meet 만나다	met 만났다	met 만났었다
read 읽다	read 읽었다	read 읽었었다	hurt 다치다	hurt 다쳤다	hurt 다쳤었다
say 말하다	said 말했다	said 말했었다	sing 노래하다	sang 노래했다	sung 노래했었다
tell 말하다 (말을 전할 때)	told 말했다	told 말했었다	pay 돈을 내다	paid 돈을 냈다	paid 돈을 냈었다
speak 말하다 (말을 주고 받을 때)	spoke 말했다	spoken 말했었다	give 주다	gave 줬다	given 줬었다
get 얻다	got 얻었다	gotten 얻었었다	run 달리다	ran 달렸다	run 달렸었다

22과에서 did를 사용하기 위해 단어에 ed를 붙여 사용했지만 예외인 단어들은 ed를 사용할 수 없으므로 모두 외워야 한다.

①	②	③	①	②	③
know 알다	knew 알았다	known 알았었다	forgive 용서하다	forgave 용서했다	forgiven 용서했었다
leave 떠나다	left 떠났다	left 떠났었다	keep 유지하다	kept 유지했다	kept 유지했었다
spend 소비하다	spent 소비했다	spent 소비했었다	mean 의미하다	meant 의미했다	meant 의미했었다
feel 느끼다	felt 느꼈다	felt 느꼈었다	stand 서다	stood 섰다	stood 섰었다
think 생각하다	thought 생각했다	thought 생각했었다	teach 가르치다	taught 가르쳤다	taught 가르쳤었다
hear 듣다	heard 들었다	heard 들었었다	drive 운전하다	drove 운전했다	driven 운전했었다
make 만들다	made 만들었다	made 만들었었다	fall 넘어지다	fell 넘어졌다	fallen 넘어졌었다
put 놓다	put 놓았다	put 놓았었다	ring 울리다	rang 울렸다	rung 울렸었다
win 이기다	won 이겼다	won 이겼었다	freeze 얼다	froze 얼었다	frozen 얼었었다
fly 날다	flew 날았다	flown 날았었다	grow 자라다	grew 자랐다	grown 자랐었다
forget 잊다	forgot 잊었다	forgotten 잊었었다	swim 헤엄치다	swam 헤엄쳤다	swum 헤엄쳤었다
ride 타다	rode 탔다	ridden 탔었다	shake 흔들다	shook 흔들었다	shaken 흔들었었다
steal 훔치다	stole 훔쳤다	stolen 훔쳤었다	hang 메달다	hung 메달았다	hung 메달았었다
throw 던지다	threw 던졌다	thrown 던졌었다	lend 빌려주다	lent 빌려줬다	lent 빌려줬었다
build 짓다	built 지었다	built 지었었다다	hold 쥐다	held 쥐었다	held 쥐었었다다
shoot 쏘다	shot 쐈다	shot 쐈었다	lie 눕다	lay 누웠다	lain 누웠었다

UNIT 23 (2) I Did (예외)
저는 ___ ㅆ어요/었어요/했어요

I

go
운동하다

I did go. → I went.
네! 저는 갔어요.   저는 갔어요.

you

sleep
자다

You did sleep. → You slept.
네! 당신은 잤어요.   당신은 잤어요.

we

fight
싸우다

We did fight. → We fought.
네! 우리는 싸웠어요.   우리는 싸웠어요.

they

eat
먹다

They did eat. → They ate.
네! 그들은 먹었어요.   그들은 먹었어요.

he

meet
만나다

He did meet her. → He met her.
네! 그는 그녀를 만났어요.   그는 그녀를 만났어요.

she

make
만들다

She did make them. → She made them.
네! 그녀가 그것들을 만들었어요.   그녀가 그것들을 만들었어요.

it

hurt
다치게 하다

It did hurt me. → It hurt me.
네! 그것이 저를 다치게 했어요.   그것이 저를 다치게 했어요.
(저에게 상처를 줬어요.)

연습문제 Unit 23

1. 번역된 문장을 참고하여 주어진 문장을 완성하시오.

1) I _____ it.
저는 그것을 알았어요.

2) We _____ dinner.
우리는 저녁을 먹었어요.

3) We _____ our car.
우리는 차를 팔았어요.

4) She _____ it.
그녀는 그것을 샀어요.

5) I _____ a house.
저는 집을 지었어요.

6) They _____ my money.
그들이 제 돈을 훔쳤어요.

7) He _____ it.
그가 그것을 했어요.

8) You _____ me.
제 말을 들었잖아요.

9) I _____ something.
저는 뭔가를 잊어버렸어요.

10) I _____ *myself*.
저는 제 자신을 가르쳤어요(독학했어요).

11) We _____ her everything.
우리는 그녀에게 모든 것을 말했어요.

12) My dad _____ for it.
우리 아빠가 돈을 냈어요.

2. 주어진 단어를 사용하여 문장을 완성하시오.

> take a picture   leave   send   come   buy   think   bring   find   lose   eat   go   choose

1) I _____ .
저는 캐나다에 갔어요.

2) _____ .
그가 왔어요.

3) _____ .
그녀는 떠났어요.

4) _____ .
그녀는 사진을 찍었어요.

5) _____ .
그는 저를 찾았어요.

6) _____ .
저는 편지를 보냈어요.

7) _____ .
그들이 이것을 가지고 왔어요.

8) _____ .
그녀는 그것을 샀어요.

9) _____ .
저는 제 핸드폰을 잃어버렸어요.

10) _____ .
저는 그것들을 먹었어요.

11) _____ .
저는 그렇게 생각했어요.

12) _____ .
그는 그녀를 선택했어요.

3. 주어진 문장에서 밑줄 친 부분을 '~했어요'의 형태로 고쳐 문장을 완성하시오.

1) I <u>buy</u> a car because I <u>need</u> it.

2) She <u>take</u> a picture and <u>bring</u> it here.

3) He <u>choose</u> her because he <u>likes</u> her.

4) I <u>write</u> a letter and <u>send</u> it to my dad.

5) I <u>meet</u> her, then <u>go</u> to the cafe to get some coffee.

4. 주어진 단어를 사용하여 '~했어요'로 문장을 만드시오.

1) (send)

2) (go)

3) (make)

4) (feel)

5) (leave)

5. 예외 단어를 사용하여 오늘 일어난 모든 일들을 쓰시오.

UNIT 24

Did I ___?
제가 ___ㅆ어요/었어요/했어요?

I — Did I

work out	I did work out. →	Did I work out?	When did I work out?
운동하다	저는 운동했어요.	제가 운동했냐고요?	제가 언제 운동했냐고요?

you — Did you

cook	You did cook. →	Did you cook?	How did you cook?
요리하다	당신은 요리했어요.	당신이 요리했어요?	어떻게 요리했어요?

we — Did we

bring	We did bring it. →	Did we bring it?	Who brought it?
가지고 오다	우리는 그것을 가져 왔어요.	우리는 그것을 가져 왔어요?	누가 그것을 가지고 왔어요?

they — Did they

come	They did come. →	Did they come?	Why did they come?
오다	그들은 왔어요.	그들은 왔어요?	그들은 왜 왔어요?

he — Did he

buy	He did buy it. →	Did he buy it?	What did he buy?
사다	그는 그것을 샀어요.	그는 그것을 샀어요?	그는 무엇을 샀어요?

she — Did she

leave	She did leave. →	Did she leave?	Who did she leave with?
떠나다	그녀는 떠났어요.	그녀는 떠났어요?	그녀는 누구랑 떠났어요?

it — Did it

work	It did work. →	Did it work?	How did you do it?
작동되다	됐어요. (작동됐어요)	됐어요? (작동됐어요?)	어떻게 하신 거예요?

연습문제　　　　　　　　　　　　　　　　　Unit 24

1. did를 사용하여 빈 칸을 채워 질문을 만드시오.

1) _____ finish it?　　2) _____ take a shower?　　3) _____ say something?
　당신은 그것을 끝냈어요?　　　그는 샤워를 했어요?　　　　　　그녀는 뭔가 말했어요?

4) _____ get to the airport?　5) _____ fight?　　6) _____ answer?
　당신은 공항에 도착했어요?　　　　　당신들은 싸웠어요?　　　　제가 대답했나요?

7) _____ come?　　8) _____ get a haircut?　　9) _____ cook yesterday?
　그들은 왔어요?　　　　　　당신은 머리를 잘랐어요?　　　　그녀는 어제 요리를 했어요?

2. did를 사용하여 대답에 맞는 질문을 완성하시오.

1) A: _____　　B: Yes, I finished it.
2) A: _____　　B: Yes, she got in the taxi.
3) A: _____　　B: Yes, he took the subway.
4) A: _____　　B: Yes, I ordered pizza.
5) A: _____　　B: Yes, they got home safe.

3. did와 when, where, who, what, how, why, which 등을 알맞게 사용하여 질문을 만드시오.

1) _____ you order it?　2) _____ Kevin get here?　3) _____ you eat for dinner?
　왜 그것을 주문했어요?　　　　케빈은 언제 도착했어요?　　　당신은 저녁으로 뭘 먹었어요?

4) _____ she know?　　5) _____ they go today?　　6) _____ you do last weekend?
　그녀가 어떻게 알았어요?　　　그들은 오늘 어디에 갔어요?　　당신은 지난 주말에 뭘 했어요?

7) _____ you get up?　　8) _____ you visit?　　9) _____ you watch yesterday?
　오늘 몇 시에 일어났어요?　　　어떤 국가를 방문했어요?　　　당신은 무슨 영화를 봤어요?

4. 순서에 맞게 나열하여 대답에 맞는 질문을 완성하시오.

1) (what, you, do, did, last Sunday)　A: _____　B: I met my buddies.
2) (at, time, go, there, did, you, what) A: _____　B: I went there at 2.
3) (get a haircut, she, when, did)　　A: _____　B: She got a haircut today.
4) (go, did, he, where, yesterday)　　A: _____　B: He went to the library.
5) (meet, how, you guys, did)　　　　A: _____　B: We met on the street.

5. did와 when, where, who, what, how, why 등을 알맞게 사용하여 대답에 맞는 질문을 완성하시오.

1) A: _____　　B: I bought a bag.
2) A: _____　　B: She got here at 7.
3) A: _____　　B: He brought his daughter.
4) A: _____　　B: I got them in Singapore.
5) A: _____　　B: I read Harry Potter.

65

UNIT 25

I did not ___

안 ___ㅆ어요/었어요/했어요 = ___지 않았어요

		did not → didn't	
I			
take a shower 샤워하다	I did take a shower. 저는 샤워를 했어요.	→	I did not take a shower. 저는 샤워를 안 했어요.
you		did not → didn't	
call 전화하다	You did call me. 당신은 저한테 전화했어요.	→	You did not call me. 당신은 저한테 전화 안 했어요.
we		did not → didn't	
agree 동의하다	We did agree. 우리는 동의했어요.	→	We did not agree. 우리는 동의하지 않았어요.
they		did not → didn't	
ride a bicycle 자전거를 타다	They did ride a bicycle. 그들은 자전거를 탔어요.	→	They did not ride a bicycle. 그들은 자전거를 타지 않았어요.
he		did not → didn't	
take a bus 버스를 타다	He did take a bus. 그는 버스를 탔어요.	→	He did not take a bus. 그는 버스를 타지 않았어요.
she		did not → didn't	
get in the cab 택시에 타다	She did get in the cab. 그녀는 택시에 탔어요.	→	She did not get in the cab. 그녀는 택시에 타지 않았어요.
it		did not → didn't	
happen 일어나다, 발생하다	It did happen. 그 (일이) 일어났어요.	→	It did not happen. (어떤 일이) 일어나지 않았어요.

연습문제 — Unit 25

1. 주어진 단어와 didn't을 사용하여 '~하지 않았어요'로 문장을 완성하시오.

> know   leave   show up   give up   get a haircut   take a picture   answer   arrive   pay

1) She _____.
그녀는 대답하지 않았어요.
2) I _____ that.
저는 그것을 몰랐어요.
3) They _____.
그들은 나타나지 않았어요.
4) We _____.
우리는 (돈을) 내지 않았어요.
5) You _____.
당신은 포기하지 않았어요.
6) He _____.
그는 사진을 찍지 않았어요.
7) My package _____ yet.
제 소포가 아직 도착하지 않았어요.
8) I _____.
저는 머리를 자르지 않았어요.
9) She _____ yet.
그녀는 아직 떠나지 않았어요.

2. didn't을 사용하여 질문에 답하시오.

1) A: Did you know that?   B: No, I didn't know that.
2) A: Did you finish your homework?   B: No, _____
3) A: Did he go to the market?   B: No, _____
4) A: Did she come here?   B: No, _____
5) A: Did they pay?   B: No, _____

3. didn't을 사용하여 질문에 답하시오.

1) A: Why did you take a picture?   B: I didn't take a picture.
2) A: How did you know?   B: _____
3) A: Where did you meet her?   B: _____
4) A: When did he show up?   B: _____
5) A: Why did she give up?   B: _____

4. didn't과 was/wasn't, 그리고 주어진 단어를 사용하여 질문에 알맞은 대답을 완성하시오.

1) A: Did you go there?   B: No, _____ go because _____ sick.
2) A: She didn't come?   B: No, _____ busy so _____ come.
3) A: Did he eat?   B: No, _____ eat because _____ hungry.
4) A: Did you guys buy it?   B: No, _____ buy it because it _____ expensive.
5) A: Did you pass the exam? B: Yes. _____ study, but _____ easy.

5. did와 did not을 사용하여 오늘의 일기를 쓰시오.

_____
_____

UNIT 26

for ___
___을/를 위해, ___동안

을/를 위해 ·· for ··

I am here for you.
저는 당신을 위해 여기에 있어요.

I did it for her.
저는 그녀를 위해서 (그것을) 했어요.

This is for you.
이것은 당신을 위한 것이에요.

This book is for studying.
이 책은 공부를 위한 것이에요.

I work for Samsung.
저는 삼성을 위해(삼성에서) 일해요.

This camera is for taking pictures.
이 카메라는 사진을 찍기 위한 것이에요.

동안 ·· for ··

For 5 minutes.
5분 동안이요.

Please wait for 10 minutes.
5분 동안 기다려 주세요.

For an hour.
한 시간 동안이요.

I waited for 2 hours.
저는 두 시간 동안 기다렸어요.

For hours.
수 시간 동안이요

I worked for hours.
저는 수 시간 동안 일했어요.

For 10 years.
10년 동안이요.

We practiced for a year.
우리는 1년 동안 연습했어요.

기타 ·· for ··

Thank you for helping me.
저를 도와주셔서 감사합니다.

I feel sorry for her.
저는 그녀가 안쓰러워요.

68

연습문제 Unit 26

1. for을 사용하여 문장을 완성하시오. (위해)

1) It is ___ me.
2) I built a house ___ my parents. *build: 짓다*
3) He works ___ Microsoft.
4) I got this ___ you.
5) I'm saving up ___ my family. *save up: (돈을) 모으다*
6) I live ___ this.
7) He makes a sacrifice ___ us. *make a sacrifice: 희생하다*
9) We are preparing ___ a job interview. *prepare: 준비하다*
9) We are waiting ___ her.

2. for + ing를 사용하여 질문에 맞는 대답을 완성하시오.

> edit photos   recycle   play video games   charge my phone   study English

1) A: What is this box for?   B: It is _____
2) A: What is this machine for?   B: It is _____
3) A: What is this book for?   B: It is _____
4) A: What is this battery for?   B: It is _____
5) A: What is this app for?   B: It is _____

3. for을 사용하여 문장을 완성하시오. (동안)

1) I played video games ___ a while. *a while: 잠시*
2) I booked a room ___ a week. *book: 예약하다*
3) We practiced ___ weeks. *weeks: 몇 주*
4) I stayed in Vietnam ___ a few days. *a few: 몇*
5) I waited ___ a long time. *long time: 오래*
6) They store it ___ a month. *store: 보관하다, 저장하다*
7) I lived in Korea ___ 20 years.
8) We talked ___ 2 hours.
9) We walked ___ 30 minutes.

4. for을 사용하여 순서에 맞게 질문에 맞는 대답을 완성하시오.

> 1) a year   2) a few minutes   3) 2 weeks   4) 5 months   5) an hour

1) A: How long did you live in Australia?   B: _____
2) A: How long did you wait for me?   B: _____
3) A: How long did he stay here?   B: _____
4) A: How long did she keep it?   B: _____
5) A: How long did they practice?   B: _____

5. for을 사용하여 문장을 완성하시오.

1) Thank you ___ come ___ .
2) Thank you ___ share ___ .
3) Thanks ___ watch ___ .
4) Thanks ___ your time.
5) I feel so sorry ___ him.
6) I am sorry ___ your loss.

UNIT 27

I am ___ing
저는 ___고 있어요

I ·· I am → I'm ··

I am studying. → I'm studying Japanese.
저는 공부하고 있어요. 저는 일본어를 공부하고 있어요

you ·· you are → you're ··

You are drinking. → You're drinking coffee.
당신은 마시고 있어요. 당신은 커피를 마시고 있어요.

we ·· we are → we're ··

We are selling. → We're selling a car.
우리는 팔고 있어요. 우리는 차를 팔고 있어요.

they ·· they are → they're ··

They are coming. → They're coming to Seoul.
그들은 오고 있어요. 그들은 서울에 오고 있어요.

*come: 오다
e로 끝나는 단어는 e를 제거

he ·· he is → he's ··

He is sleeping. → He's sleeping at home now.
그는 자고 있어요. 그는 지금 집에서 자고 있어요.

she ·· she is → she's ··

She is walking. → She's walking around.
그녀는 걷고 있어요. 그녀는 주변을 걷고 있어요.

it ·· it is → it's ··

It is raining. → It's raining outside.
비가 내리고 있어요. 밖에 비가 내리고 있어요.

예외 ·· 미래형으로 사용 가능 ··

I am working. → I am working tomorrow.
저는 내일 일해요.

70

연습문제 — Unit 27

1. am, are, is와 ing를 알맞게 사용하여 빈 칸을 채워 문장을 완성하시오.

1) I ___ work ___ at the moment. 저는 지금 (이 순간) 일하고 있어요.
2) He ___ just exaggerate ___. 그는 그냥 과장하고 있어요.
3) We ___ compare ___. 우리는 비교하고 있어요.
4) She ___ do ___ the dishes. 그녀는 설거지를 하고 있어요.
5) We ___ sing ___ at home. 우리는 집에서 노래하고 있어요.
6) I ___ do ___ the laundry. 저는 빨래를 하고 있어요.
7) He ___ come ___ here now. 그는 지금 여기에 오고 있어요.
8) It ___ rain ___ there. 거기에 비가 내리고 있어요.
9) You ___ lie ___ to me. 당신은 저한테 거짓말하고 있어요.

2. ing를 사용하여 다음을 번역하시오.

1) 저는 지금 자고 있어요.
2) 저는 지금 집에서 노래를 부르고 있어요.
3) 그녀는 집에서 친구와 티비를 보고 있어요.
4) 우리는 내일 일해요.
5) 그녀는 다음 주에 그녀의 친구들과 여기에 와요.

3. am, are, is와 ing를 알맞게 사용하여 빈 칸을 채워 문장을 완성하시오.

1) My parents ___ come ___. 오다
2) Kevin ___ look ___ for a job. 일을 찾다
3) Nick ___ get ___ drunk. 취하다
4) Sam ___ have ___ fun. 재미있게 놀다
5) Jane's friend ___ get ___ on a plane. 비행기에 타다
6) Your dog ___ bark ___. 짖다
7) His dad ___ fix ___ a fan. 선풍기를 고치다
8) My co-workers ___ work ___ hard. 열심히 일하다
9) A girl ___ take ___ a picture. 사진을 찍다

4. 다음을 영어로 번역하시오.

1) 제 남편은 사진을 찍고 있어요.
2) 제 부모님은 스페인에서 일하고 있어요.
3) Tom은 서점에서 책을 찾고 있어요.
4) John은 공항에서 비행기를 타고 있어요.
5) Emily는 지금 그녀의 남자친구와 재미있게 놀고 있어요.

5. am, are, is + ing를 사용하여 질문에 맞는 답을 쓰시오.

1) What are you doing today?
2) What are you doing tomorrow?
3) What are you doing this weekend?

UNIT 28

Am I ___ing?
저는 ___고 있어요?

I — I am → am I?

I am focusing.
저는 집중하고 있어요.

Am I focusing?
(제가) 집중하고 있냐고요?
(제가) 집중하고 있나요?

How am I focusing?
제가 어떻게 집중하고 있냐고요?
제가 어떻게 집중하고 있나요?

you — you are → are you?

You are thinking.
당신은 생각하고 있어요.

Are you thinking?
당신은 생각하고 있어요?

What are you thinking?
당신은 뭐를 생각하고 있어요?

we — we are → are we?

We are laughing.
우리는 웃고 있어요.

Are we laughing?
우리는 웃고 있어요?

Why are we laughing?
우리는 왜 웃고 있어요?

they — they are → were they?

They are guessing.
그들은 추측하고 있어요.

Are they guessing?
그들은 추측하고 있어요?

What are they guessing?
그들은 무엇을 추측하고 있어요?

he — he is → is he?

He is talking.
그는 얘기하고 있어요.

Is he talking?
그는 얘기하고 있어요?

Who is he talking to?
그는 누구한테 얘기하고 있어요?

she — she is → is she?

She is walking.
그녀는 걷고 있어요.

Is she walking?
그녀는 걷고 있어요?

Who is she walking with?
그녀는 누구랑 걷고 있어요?

it — it is → it's

It is falling.
그것이 떨어지고 있어요.

Is it falling?
그것이 떨어지고 있어요?

What is falling?
무엇이 떨어지고 있어요?

연습문제　　　　　　　　　　　　　　　　　　　Unit 28

1. am, are, is와 ing를 알맞게 사용하여 빈 칸을 채워 질문을 완성하시오.

1) _____ you joke_____?　　2) _____ he laugh_____?　　3) _____ he flirt_____ with me?
joke: 농담하다　　　　　　　　laugh: 웃다　　　　　　　　　　flirt: 추파를 던지다

4) _____ you have_____ fun?　5) _____ I dream_____?　　6) _____ you leave_____ tomorrow?
have fun: 재미있게 놀다　　　　dream: 꿈을 꾸다　　　　　　　leave: 떠나다

7) _____ it snow_____ now?　8) _____ she get_____ in a taxi?　9) _____ he get_____ on the subway?
snow: 눈이 내리다　　　　　　　get in: 타다　　　　　　　　　　get on: 타다

2. 대답에 맞게 질문하시오.

1) _____　→　Yes, I'm coming.
2) _____　→　Yes, she's having fun.
3) _____　→　Yes, I'm getting on the bus.
4) _____　→　Yes, it's raining now.
5) _____　→　Yes, he's leaving tomorrow.

3. am, are, is와 ing를 알맞게 사용하여 질문을 완성하시오.

1) Why _____ you cry_____?　　2) What _____ you do_____?　　3) Where _____ he go_____?

4) _____ they come_____?　5) _____ you watch_____?　6) _____ you meet_____ today?
→ 그들은 언제 와요?　　　　　→ 무슨 영화를 보고 있어요?　　→ 당신은 오늘 누구를 만나요?

7) _____ we meet_____?　8) _____ you do_____?　　9) _____ he listen_____ to?
→ 우리는 몇 시에 만나요?　　→ 당신은 어떻게 지내고 있어요?　→ 그는 어떤 종류의 음악을 듣고 있어요?

4. when, where, who, what, how, why와 ing를 사용하여 대답에 맞게 질문하시오.

1) _____　→　I am studying now.
2) _____　→　I'm studying at home.
3) _____　→　I'm studying English.
4) _____　→　I'm studying with my girlfriend.
5) _____　→　I'm studying because I have an exam tomorrow.

5. when, where, who, what, how, why를 사용하여 질문과 답변을 만드시오.

1) _____　→　_____
2) _____　→　_____
3) _____　→　_____
4) _____　→　_____
5) _____　→　_____

UNIT 29

I am not ___ing
안 ___고 있어요 = ___지 않고 있어요

I — I am not → I'm not

exaggerate 과장하다
I am exaggerating. 저는 과장하고 있어요. → I am not exaggerating. 저는 과장하고 있지 않아요.

---

you — you are not → you aren't

support 지지하다
You are supporting us. 당신은 우리를 지지하고 있어요. → You are not supporting us. 당신은 우리를 지지하고 있지 않아요.

---

we — we are not → we aren't

consider 고려하다
We are considering it. 우리는 그것을 고려하고 있어요. → We are not considering it. 우리는 그것을 고려하고 있지 않아요.

---

they — they are not → they aren't

convince 납득시키다
They are convincing her. 그들은 그녀를 납득시키고 있어요. → They are not convincing her. 그들은 그녀를 납득시키고 있지 않아요.

---

he — he is not → he isn't

realize 깨닫다
He is realizing it. 그는 그것을 깨닫고 있어요. → He is not realizing it. 그는 그것을 깨닫고 있지 않아요.

---

she — she is not → she isn't

concentrate 집중하다
She is concentrating. 그녀는 집중하고 있어요. → She is not concentrating. 그녀는 집중하고 있지 않아요.

---

it — it is not → it isn't

pour 쏟아지다
It is pouring. (비가) 쏟아지고 있어요. → It is not pouring. (비가) 쏟아지고 있지 않아요.

연습문제   Unit 29

1. am, are, is와 not, 그리고 ing를 알맞게 사용하여 '~하고 있지 않아요'와 같이 완성하시오.

1) He _____ concentrate _____ .
concentrate: 집중하다

2) He _____ support _____ them.
support: 지지하다

3) I _____ exaggerate _____ .
exaggerate: 과장하다

4) We _____ convince _____ her.
convince: 설득하다

5) She _____ consider _____ it.
consider: 고려하다

6) I _____ eat _____ anything.
eat: 먹다

7) They _____ try _____ enough.
try: 시도하다

8) You _____ do _____ anything.
do: 하다

9) It _____ work _____ at all.
work: 작동하다

2. am, are, is와 not, 그리고 ing를 알맞게 사용하여 질문에 답하시오.

1) Is she trying hard enough? → No, _____

2) Are they supporting him? → No, _____

3) Are you concentrating? → No, _____

4) Are you doing something right now? → No, _____

5) Is it working properly? → No, _____

3. Are you ~ing?를 사용하여 질문, I'm not ~ing를 사용하여 대화를 만드시오.

1) _____ → _____
2) _____ → _____
3) _____ → _____
4) _____ → _____
5) _____ → _____

4. 주어진 단어를 순서대로 사용하여 질문에 알맞은 대답을 완성하시오.

((work, Sunday)　(sleep, not tired)　(come, busy)　(rain, cloudy)　(cry, not happy))

1) Are you working tomorrow?　B: No, _____ because _____

2) Is he sleeping?　B: No, _____ because _____

3) Are they coming now?　B: No, _____ because _____

4) Is it raining outside?　B: No, _____ but _____

5) Is she crying?　B: No, _____ but _____

UNIT 30

I was ___ing
___고 있었어요

I — was

wonder 궁금해하다
I was wondering.
저는 궁금해하고 있었어요.
→ I was wondering about it, too.
저도 그것에 대해서 궁금해하고 있었어요.

you — were

complain 불평하다
You were complaining.
당신은 불평하고 있었어요.
→ You were complaining about it.
당신은 그것에 대해서 불평하고 있었어요.

we — were

unpack 짐을 풀다
We were unpacking.
우리는 짐을 풀고 있었어요.
→ We were unpacking our stuff.
우리는 (우리 물건이 든) 짐을 풀고 있었어요.

they — were

expect 기대하다
They were expecting it.
그들은 (그것을) 기대하고 있었어요.
→ They were expecting something.
그들은 무언가를 기대하고 있었어요.

he — was

take a shower 샤워하다
He was taking a shower.
그는 샤워를 하고 있었어요.
→ He was taking a shower in the bathroom.
그는 화장실에서 샤워를 하고 있었어요.

she — was

take a bath 목욕하다
She was taking a bath.
그녀는 목욕을 하고 있었어요.
→ She was taking a bath at 2 in the morning.
그녀는 새벽 2시에 목욕을 하고 있었어요.

it — was

ring (벨이) 울리다
It was ringing.
그것이 울리고 있었어요.
→ The phone was ringing constantly.
그 핸드폰이 끊임없이 울리고 있었어요.

연습문제 Unit 30

1. was, were과 ing를 알맞게 사용하여 빈 칸을 채워 질문을 완성하시오.

1) I ____ look ____ for you.
   look for: 찾다
2) He ____ fight ____ with her.
   fight: 싸우다
3) She ____ yell ____ at him.
   yell: 소리치다
4) You ____ take ____ a bath.
   take a bath: 목욕하다
5) We ____ take ____ a picture.
   take a picture: 사진을 찍다
6) They ____ take ____ a walk.
   take a walk: 산책하다
7) I ____ take ____ a nap.
   take a nap: 낮잠을 자다
8) My brother ____ take ____ a class.
   take a class: 수강하다, 수업을 듣다
9) Jessica ____ play ____ tennis.
   play tennis: 테니스를 치다

2. 주어진 문장을 영어로 번역하시오.

1) 저는 제 남동생을 찾고 있었어요.
2) 그녀는 학교에서 수업을 듣고 있었어요.
3) 우리는 어제 골프를 치고 있었어요.
4) 그들은 새벽 두 시에 산책을 하고 있었어요.
5) 당신은 5시에 낮잠을 자고 있었어요.

3. 주어진 단어와 was, were, 그리고 ing를 알맞게 사용하여 문장을 완성하시오.

1) (in, I, a walk, take, the park) →
2) (class, she, a, take, history) →
3) (we, wait, so long, for, you) →
4) (his, Kevin, room, play, the guitar, in) →
5) (Steve and Sam, together, play, golf) →

4. was, were과 ing를 알맞게 사용하여 질문에 대답하시오.

1) Were you taking a picture? → Yes,
2) Was she taking a walk in the park? → Yes,
3) Were they waiting for you? → Yes,
4) Were you listening to me? → Yes,
5) Was he taking a bath? → Yes,

5. was와 ing를 사용하여 질문에 자유롭게 답하시오.

1) What were you doing there? →
2) I called you three times. →
3) Why didn't you pick up the phone? →
4) Why did you ignore my message? →
5) Why did you not answer me? →

UNIT 31

Was I ___ing?
___고 있었어요?

I — I was → was I

I was listening.
저는 듣고 있었어요.

Was I listening?
(제가) 듣고 있었냐고요?
(제가) 듣고 있었나요?

What was I listening to?
제가 무엇을 듣고 있었냐고요?
제가 무엇을 듣고 있었나요?

you — you were → were you

You were working.
당신은 일하고 있었어요.

Were you working?
당신은 일하고 있었어요?

Where were you working?
당신은 어디에서 일하고 있었어요?

we — we were → were we

We were waiting.
우리는 기다리고 있었어요.

Were we waiting?
우리는 기다리고 있었어요?

How long were we waiting?
우리는 얼마나 오래 기다리고 있었어요?

they — they were → were they

They were expecting it.
그들은 그것을 기대하고 있었어요.

Were they expecting it?
그들은 그것을 기대하고 있었어요?

What were they expecting?
그들은 무엇을 기대하고 있었어요?

he — he was → was he

He was asking.
그는 물어보고 있었어요.

Was he asking?
그는 물어보고 있었어요?

Who was he asking?
그는 누구한테 물어보고 있었어요?

she — she was → was she

She was reading.
그녀는 읽고 있었어요.

Was she reading?
그녀는 읽고 있었어요?

Which book was she reading?
그녀는 어느 책을 읽고 있었어요?

it — it was → was it

It was falling.
그것이 떨어지고 있었어요.

Was it falling?
그것이 떨어지고 있었어요?

What was falling?
무엇이 떨어지고 있었어요?

연습문제 — Unit 31

1. was, were과 ing를 알맞게 사용하여 질문을 완성하시오.

1) _____ you smoke _____ ?   2) _____ he teach _____ ?   3) _____ I snore _____ ?
   smoke: 담배를 피우다   teach: 가르치다   snore: 코를 골다

4) _____ she drive _____ a car?   5) _____ you ride _____ a bicycle?   6) _____ they avoid _____ you?
   drive: 운전하다   ride a bicycle: 자전거를 타다   avoid: 피하다

7) _____ they record _____ a video?   8) _____ he tell _____ the truth?   9) _____ you hold _____ it?
   record: 녹화하다   tell the truth: 사실을 말하다   hold: 잡다, 쥐다

2. was, were과 ing를 사용하여 질문을 완성하시오.

1) What _____ you do _____ ?   2) Where _____ you go _____ ?   3) Who _____ you wait _____ for?

4) _____ you watch _____ ?   5) _____ you play _____ ?   6) _____ you make _____ ?
   → 어느 드라마/방송을 보고 있었어요?   → 무슨 게임을 하고 있었어요?   → 뭐를 만들고 있었어요?

7) _____ he drink _____ ?   8) _____ she read _____ ?   9) _____ he listen _____ ?
   → 그는 무슨 차를 마시고 있었어요?   → 그녀는 무슨 책을 읽고 있었어요?   → 그는 어떤 종류의 음악을 듣고 있었어요?

3. 주어진 문장을 번역하시오.

1) 뭐를 하고 있었어요? →
2) 저를 기다리고 있었어요? →
3) 어디에서 기다리고 있었어요? →
4) 뭐를 생각하고 있었어요? →
5) 그는 여기에서 낮잠을 자고 있었어요? →

4. 주어진 단어와 was와 were를 활용하여 대답에 맞는 질문을 만드시오.

1) What were you doing?   → I was cooking.
2) What _____   → I was cooking bacon.
3) Where _____   → I was cooking in the kitchen.
4) Who _____   → I was cooking by myself.
5) Why _____   → I was cooking because I was hungry.

5. when, where, who, what, how, why와 were you + ing를 사용하여 질문과 답변을 만드시오.

1) _____ →
2) _____ →
3) _____ →
4) _____ →
5) _____ →

UNIT 32 I was not ___ing
안 ___고 있었어요 = ___지 않고 있었어요

I ········· was not → wasn't

rest
쉬다
I was resting. → I was not resting.
저는 쉬고 있었어요. 저는 안 쉬고 있었어요.

you ········· were not → weren't

stare
쳐다보다
You were staring at me. → You were not staring at me.
당신은 저를 쳐다보고 있었어요. 당신은 저를 안 쳐다보고 있었어요.

we ········· were not → weren't

play a game
게임을 하다
We were playing a game. → We were not playing a game.
우리는 게임을 하고 있었어요. 우리는 게임을 안 하고 있었어요.

they ········· were not → weren't

pray
기도하다
They were praying. → They were not praying.
그들은 기도하고 있었어요. 그들은 기도를 안 하고 있었어요.

he ········· was not → wasn't

hope
바라다
He was hoping. → He was not hoping.
그는 바라고 있었어요. 그는 바라고 있지 않았어요.

she ········· was not → wasn't

shake
흔들다
She was shaking it. → She was not shaking it.
그녀는 그것을 흔들고 있었어요. 그녀는 그것을 안 흔들고 있었어요.

it ········· was not → wasn't

shine
반짝이다
It was shining. → It was not shining.
그것은 반짝이고 있었어요. 그것은 반짝이고 있지 않았어요.

연습문제 Unit 32

1. wasn't ~ing, weren't ~ing를 알맞게 사용하여 질문을 완성하시오.

1) It _____ work _____ properly.
   work: 작동되다
2) I _____ stare _____ at you.
   stare: 노려보다
3) I _____ look _____ for you.
   look for: 찾다
4) She _____ take _____ a nap.
   take a nap: 낮잠을 자다
5) You _____ talk _____ to me.
   talk: 얘기하다
6) I _____ look _____ at it.
   look at: 보다
7) He _____ wait _____ for me.
   wait: 기다리다
8) My parents _____ listen _____ .
   listen: 듣다
9) My friend _____ enjoy _____ it.
   enjoy: 즐기다

2. wasn't ~ing를 알맞게 사용하여 질문에 답하시오.

1) Were you listening? → _____
2) Were you staring at me? → _____
3) Was he taking a nap? → _____
4) Was she looking for me? → _____
5) Were your parents waiting for you? → _____

3. wasn't ~ing와 was을 알맞게 사용하여 질문에 답하시오.

1) A: Were you taking a shower? → B: No, I wasn't taking a shower. I was watching TV.
2) A: Was she waiting for you? → B: No, _____ . She
3) A: Were you studying at home? → B: No, _____ . I
4) A: Was Steve taking a nap? → B: No, _____ . He
5) A: Was your dad fishing? → B: No, _____ . He

4. was와 wasn't ~ing를 활용하여 대화를 만드시오.

1) _____ → _____
2) _____ → _____
3) _____ → _____
4) _____ → _____
5) _____ → _____

5. wasn't ~ing을 활용하여 질문에 답하시오.

1) What were you buying? → _____ anything.
2) Where were you going? → _____ anywhere.
3) Who were you meeting with? → _____ with anyone.
4) Who were you drinking with? → _____ with anybody.
5) Which tools were you using? → _____ any tools.

UNIT 33

I am going to ___
저는 ___ㄹ 거예요/을 거예요

I — going to → gonna

be - 되다	be - 지다	do - 하다

I am going to be a pilot.
저는 비행기 조종사가 될 거예요.

I am going to be busy.
저는 바빠질 거예요.

I'm going to rest.
저는 쉴 거예요.

you — going to → gonna

You are going to be a cook.
당신은 요리사가 될 거예요.

You are going to be rich.
당신은 부유해질 거예요.

You are going to survive.
당신은 살아남을 거예요.

we — going to → gonna

We are going to be soldiers.
우리는 군인들이 될 거예요.

We are going to be strong.
우리는 강해질 거예요.

We are going to book it.
우리는 그것을 예약할 거예요.

they — going to → gonna

They are going to be adults.
그들은 어른들이 될 거예요.

They are going to be old.
그들은 나이가 들거예요.

They are going to stay.
그들은 머무를 거예요.

he — going to → gonna

He is going to be a developer.
그는 개발자가 될 거예요.

He is going to be lazy.
그는 게을러 질 거예요.

He is going to talk.
그가 얘기할 거예요.

she — going to → gonna

She is going to be a painter.
그녀는 화가가 될 거예요.

She is going to be alright.
그녀는 괜찮아질 거예요.

She is going to come.
그녀가 올 거예요.

it — going to → gonna

It is going to be a busy day.
바쁜 날이 될 거예요.

It is going to be easy.
그것은 쉬울 거예요.

It is going to happen.
그것이 일어날 거예요.

연습문제 — Unit 33

1. be going to를 사용하여 문장을 완성하시오.

1) She _____ a flight attendant.   2) You _____ win.   3) They _____ 19.
   flight attendant: 승무원   win: 이기다   19: 19살

4) We _____ build a house.   5) I _____ a professor.   6) He _____ strong.
   build: 짓다   professor: 교수   strong: 강하다

7) It _____ dark.   8) I _____ grab it.   9) Everything _____ fine.
   dark: 어둡다   grab: 붙잡다   fine: 괜찮다, 좋다

2. be going to를 사용하여 주어진 문장을 번역하시오.

1) 우리는 괜찮아질 거예요.   →
2) 저는 여기에서 살 거예요.   →
3) 그녀가 그를 도울 거예요.   →
4) 저는 가수가 될 거예요.   →
5) 그들이 올 거예요.   →

3. 주어진 단어와 be going to를 알맞게 사용하여 문장을 완성하시오.

1) (buy) → I need a computer, so _____
2) (cook) → I'm hungry, so _____ something.
3) (come back, at 10) → We're going to leave at 7, and _____
4) (cold, at night) → It's going to be hot in the morning, and _____
5) (get, some sleep) → He's going to take a shower, and then _____

4. be going to를 사용하여 질문에 자유롭게 답하시오.

1) What are you going to do today?   →
2) Where are you going to do it?   →
3) Who are you going to do it with?   →
4) When are you going to do it?   →
5) And then, what are you going to do?   → And then,

5. be going to를 사용하여 내일 무엇을 할 것인지 쓰시오.

1)
2)
3)

UNIT 34 Are you going to ___?
ㄹ 거예요/을 거예요?

I ········· I am → am I? ·········

get married — Am I going to get married? → When am I going to get married?
결혼하다 — 저는 결혼하게 될까요? — 저는 언제 결혼하게 될까요?

you ········· you are → are you? ·········

leave — Are you going to leave? → Who are you going to leave with?
떠나다 — (당신은) 떠나실 거예요? — (당신은) 누구랑 떠나실 거예요?

we ········· we are → are we? ·········

play a game — Are we going to play a game? → Where are we going to play a game?
게임을 하다 — 우리는 게임을 할 거예요? — 우리는 어디에서 게임을 할 거예요?

they ········· they are → are they? ·········

prepare — Are they going to prepare? → When are they going to prepare?
준비하다 — 그들은 준비할 거예요? — 그들은 언제 준비할 거예요?

he ········· he is → is he? ·········

stay — Is he going to stay here? → How long is he going to stay here?
머무르다 — 그는 여기에서 머무를 거예요? — (그는) 얼마나 오래 여기에서 머무를 거예요?

she ········· she is → is she ·········

move in — Is she going to move in? → What day is she going to move in?
이사오다 — 그녀는 이사 올 거예요? — (그녀는) 무슨 요일에 이사 올 거예요?

it ········· it is → is it ·········

explode — Is it going to explode? → Why is it going to explode?
폭발하다 — 그것이 폭발할 거예요? — 그것은 왜 폭발할 거예요?

연습문제 — Unit 34

1. 주어진 단어와 be going to를 알맞게 사용하여 질문을 완성하시오.

1) _____ you _____ a pilot?　2) _____ she _____ bring it?　3) _____ they _____ stay here?
　pilot: 비행기 조종사　　　　　bring: 가지고 오다　　　　　stay: 머무르다, 지내다

4) _____ we _____ leave soon?　5) _____ she _____ alright?　6) _____ you _____ look after her?
　leave: 떠나다　　　　　alright: 괜찮다　　　　　look after: 돌보다

7) _____ it _____ chilly?　8) _____ you _____ follow me?　9) _____ your dad _____ come in?
　chilly: 쌀쌀하다　　　　　follow: 따라가다/오다　　　　　come in: 들어오다

2. be going to를 사용하여 대답에 맞게 질문하시오.

1) _____ → Yes, I'm going to stay here.
2) _____ → Yes, she's going to move there.
3) _____ → Yes, they are going to be here.
4) _____ → Yes, I'm going to be there.
5) _____ → Yes, my grandmother is going to visit me.

3. be going to를 알맞게 사용하여 질문을 완성하시오.

1) What _____ you _____ do?　　　　6) Where _____ you _____ put it?
2) Who _____ you _____ meet?　　　 7) How _____ you _____ fix it?
3) What _____ you _____ buy?　　　 8) What color _____ you _____ choose?
4) When _____ he _____ arrive?　　 9) What car _____ she _____ drive?
5) Which one _____ we _____ use?　10) At what time _____ you _____ leave?

4. 주어진 단어와 be going to를 알맞게 사용하여 질문하시오.

1) What are you going to do tomorrow? → I'm going to meet a friend tomorrow.
2) What _____ → I'm going to Busan with her.
3) At what time _____ → We are going to leave at 5.
4) How _____ → We are going to take the KTX.
5) How long _____ → We are staying for a night.

5. when, where, who, what, how, why와 be going to를 사용하여 질문과 답변을 만드시오.

1) _____ → _____
2) _____ → _____
3) _____ → _____

85

UNIT 35

I'm not going to ___
(안 ___ㄹ 거예요/을 거예요 = ___지 않을 거예요)

I
going to → gonna

I am not going to be a journalist.
저는 기자가 되지 않을 거예요.

I am not going to be upset.
저는 화를 내지 않을 거예요.

I'm not going to lie.
저는 거짓말하지 않을 거예요.

you
going to → gonna

You are not going to be a loser.
당신은 실패자가 되지 않을 거예요.

You are not going to be safe.
당신은 안전하지 않을 거예요.

You're not going to find out.
당신은 찾아내지 않을 거예요.

we
going to → gonna

We are not going to be a team.
우리는 팀이 되지 않을 거예요.

We are not going to be polite.
우리는 공손하지 않을 거예요.

We're not going to give up.
우리는 포기하지 않을 거예요.

they
going to → gonna

They are not going to be musicians.
그들은 음악가가 되지 않을 거예요.

They are not going to be comfortable.
그들은 편하지 않을 거예요.

They're not going to sign up.
그들은 가입하지 않을 거예요.

he
going to → gonna

He is not going to be a movie star.
그는 영화배우가 되지 않을 거예요.

He is not going to be fat.
그는 뚱뚱해지지 않을 거예요.

He's not going to shut up.
그는 입을 다물지 않을 거예요.

she
going to → gonna

She is not going to be a princess.
그녀는 공주가 되지 않을 거예요.

She is not going to be insane.
그녀는 미치지 않을 거예요.

She's not going to calm down.
그녀는 진정하지 않을 거예요.

it
going to → gonna

It is not going to be a problem.
그것은 문제가 되지 않을 거예요.

It is not going to be different.
그것은 다르지 않을 거예요.

It's not going to happen.
(그런 일은) 안 일어날 거예요.

연습문제 Unit 35

1. not going to를 사용하여 문장을 완성하시오.

1) I _____ a pilot. 2) She _____ come. 3) They _____ stay here.
4) We _____ leave. 5) It _____ alright. 6) He _____ there.
7) It _____ cold. 8) I _____ use it. 9) Lisa _____ live here.

2. not going to를 사용하여 질문에 맞게 답하시오.

1) Are you going to stay here? →
2) Is she really going to leave in April? →
3) Is your mom going to visit you today? →
4) Is it going to be hot anytime soon? →
5) Are they going to come or not? →

3. not going to를 사용하여 질문에 맞게 답하시오.

1) Are you coming home tomorrow? →
2) Are you working this weekend? →
3) Is she joining us? →
4) Is he moving out soon? →
5) Are we giving up? →

4. be not going to를 알맞게 사용하여 질문하시오.

1) What are you going to do about it? → _____ anything about it.
2) What are you going to tell her? → _____ anything.
3) When are you going to start? → _____ anytime soon.
4) Who are you going to meet? → _____ anyone.
5) Why are you going to quit? →

5. going to를 사용하여 질문, not going to를 사용하여 답변을 만드시오.

1) _____ →
2) _____ →
3) _____ →
4) _____ →
5) _____ →

UNIT 36

I will ___
제가 ___ㄹ게요/을게요, 꼭/분명히 ___ㄹ/을 거예요

I

I will → I'll

be - 되다

I will be your guardian.
저는 당신의 수호자가 될게요.

be - 지다

I will be free.
저는 자유로워질 거예요.

do - 하다

I will call you back.
제가 다시 (전화를) 걸게요.

you

you will → you'll

You will be a professional.
당신은 프로가 될 거예요.

You will be fine.
당신은 괜찮아질 거예요.

You will regret it.
당신은 그것을 후회할 거예요.

we

we will → we'll

We will be experts.
우리는 전문가들이 될 거예요.

We will be independent.
우리는 독립적이게 될 거예요.

We will take care of it.
우리가 그것을 처리할게요.

they

they will → they'll

They will be colleagues.
그들은 동료가 될 거예요.

They will be extraordinary.
그들은 비범해 질 거예요.

They will get over it.
그들은 그것을 극복할 거예요.

he

he will → he'll

He will be an architect.
그는 건축가가 될 거예요.

He will be here soon.
그는 곧 이곳에 있게 될 거예요 (올 거예요).

He will give her a ride.
그가 그녀를 태워다 줄 거예요.

she

she will → she'll

She will be a workaholic.
그녀는 일 중독자가 될 거예요.

She will be there.
그녀는 그곳에 있게 될 거예요 (갈 거예요).

She will look it up.
그녀가 찾아(검색해) 볼 거예요.

it

it will → it'll

It will be a huge opportunity.
그것은 거대한 기회가 될 거예요.

It will be bizarre.
그것은 특이할 거예요.

It will hurt you.
그것이 당신을 상처입힐 거예요.

연습문제 — Unit 36

1. will을 사용하여 문장을 완성하시오.

1) I _____ figure it out.
figure out: 알아내다, 해결하다

2) She _____ invite everyone.
invite: 초대하다

3) He _____ give you a ride.
give a ride: 태워 주다

4) You _____ regret it.
regret: 후회하다

5) It _____ stop soon.
stop: 멈추다

6) I _____ get rid of it.
get rid of: 제거하다

7) They _____ figure it out.
figure it out: 해결하다

8) I _____ take care of it.
take care: 돌보다, 처리하다

9) I _____ call you later.
call: 전화를 걸다, 부르다

2. will과 주어진 단어를 사용하여 질문에 맞게 답하시오.

> get rid of   do   invite   give you a ride   figure out

1) When are you going to do it? → _____ later.
2) Who are you going to invite? → _____ everybody.
3) How am I going back home? → Don't worry. I _____
4) I don't need it. → Then, I _____
5) I think she is in trouble. → It's okay. She _____

3. will과 주어진 단어를 사용하여 문장을 완성하시오.

> take care of it   look it up   treat   show you   fun

1) I can't hang out this weekend. → Oh, come on! Why not? It _____
2) Can you show me? → Sure, I can. But I _____ in a bit.
3) I'm in trouble. → Don't worry about it. Your dad _____
4) What does that mean? → I don't know. I _____
5) I can't afford it. → Don't worry about the money. It _____ my

4. will을 사용하여 여러분의 목표를 쓰시오.

1)
2)
3)
4)
5)
6)
7)
8)
9)
10)

UNIT 37

Will you ___?
(___해 줄래요?, ___할래요?, ___할까요?)

I ·· I will → will I? ··

get a refund 환불받다	Will I get a refund? 제가 환불을 받게 될까요? 제가 환불을 받게 되냐고요?	→	When will I get a refund? 제가 언제 환불을 받게 될까요? 제가 언제 환불을 받게 되냐고요?

you ·· you will → will you? ··

marry ~와 결혼하다	Will you marry me? 저와 결혼해 줄래요?	→	Who will you marry? 당신은 누구랑 결혼할래요?

we ·· we will → will we? ··

die 죽다	Will we die eventually? 우리가 결국 죽을까요?	→	Why will we die? (우리가) 왜 죽을까요?

they ·· they will → will they? ··

quit 그만두다	Will they quit? 그들이 그만둘까요?	→	When will they quit? (그들이) 언제 그만둘까요?

he ·· he will → will he? ··

come back 돌아오다	Will he come back? 그가 돌아올까요?	→	What day will he come back? 그는 무슨 요일에 돌아올까요?

she ·· she will → will she? ··

cheat 바람을 피우다	Will she cheat on me? 그녀가 저를 두고 바람을 피울까요?	→	What time will she arrive? 그녀가 몇 시에 도착할까요?

it ·· it will → will it? ··

fit (크기가) 맞다	Will it fit me? 그것이 저한테 맞을까요?	→	What size will fit? 무슨 사이즈가 맞을까요?

연습문제 Unit 37

1. will you를 사용하여 문장을 완성하시오.

1) _____ turn on the light? 2) _____ keep it down? 3) _____ put on a shirt?
   turn on: 켜다   keep down: 조용히 하다   put on: 입다

4) _____ turn it off? 5) _____ give me a ride? 6) _____ please stop?
   turn off: 끄다   give a ride: 태워 주다   stop: 멈추다

7) _____ marry me? 8) _____ be my girlfriend? 9) _____ recommend a place?
   marry: ~와 결혼하다   be: 되다, 있다   recommend: 추천하다

2. will을 사용하여 대답에 맞는 질문을 완성하시오.

1) _____ → Sure. I will give you a ride.
2) _____ → Absolutely. I will help you. Don't worry about it, buddy.
3) _____ → For sure. I will turn off the light.
4) _____ → I'm sorry. I will keep it down.
5) _____ → Okay. I will stop.

3. will을 알맞게 사용하여 다음을 번역하시오.

1) 당신을 좋아해요. 저랑 사귈래요?   → _____
2) 너무 추워요. 에어컨을 꺼 줄래요?   → _____
3) 저는 그들이 그리워요. 그들이 언제 올까요?   → _____
4) 벌써 3시예요. 그것은 얼마나 오래 걸릴까요?   → _____
5) 그는 선택해야 해요. 그는 어떤 것을 선택할까요?   → _____

4. when, where, who, what, how, why와 will을 알맞게 사용하여 질문하시오.

1) What will you do today?   → I will go shopping.
2) Where _____   → I will go to the mall.
3) Who _____   → I will go there with my roommate.
4) What _____   → I don't know yet. Maybe some clothes?
5) How much _____   → I will probably spend about $100.

5. will을 사용하여 질문과 답변을 만드시오.

1) Will you wait for me?   → Of course, I will wait for you. Take your time.
2) _____   → _____
3) _____   → _____
4) _____   → _____
5) _____   → _____

UNIT 38

I will not ___
(저는 절대 ___지 않을 거예요)

I ──────── I will not → I won't ────────

forgive
용서하다 | I will not forgive you.
저는 당신을 용서하지 않을 거예요. → I won't forgive you.

you ──────── you will not → you won't ────────

regret
후회하다 | You will not regret it.
당신은 그것을 후회하지 않을 거예요. → You won't regret it.

we ──────── we will not → we won't ────────

let ( ) down
( )를 실망시키다 | We will not let you down.
우리는 당신을 실망시키지 않을 거예요. → We won't let you down.

they ──────── they will not → they won't ────────

accept
받아들이다 | They will not accept us.
그들은 우리를 받아들이지 않을 거예요. → They won't accept us.

he ──────── he will not → he won't ────────

ask ( ) out
( )에게 데이트를 신청하다 | He will not ask you out.
그는 당신에게 데이트를 신청하지 않을 거예요. → He won't ask you out.

she ──────── she will not → she won't ────────

go out with
~와 사귀다 | She will not go out with you.
그녀는 당신과 사귀지 않을 거예요. → She won't go out with you.

it ──────── it will not → it won't ────────

difficult
어렵다 | It will not be difficult.
그것은 어렵지 않을 거예요. → It won't be difficult.

연습문제 — Unit 38

1. will not을 사용하여 문장을 완성하시오.

1) I _____ give up.
give up: 포기하다

2) They _____ forget it.
forget: 잊다

3) I _____ let you down.
let down: 기대를 저버리다 (실망시키다)

4) We _____ ditch you.
ditch: 버리다

5) She _____ text you back.
text back: (문자메세지에) 답장하다

6) He _____ take your advice.
take advice: 충고를 받아들이다

7) I _____ hesitate.
hesitate: 망설이다

8) It _____ hurt you.
hurt: 상처입히다

9) It _____ happen again.
happen: (어떤 일이) 일어나다

2. will not을 사용하여 질문에 답하시오.

1) Will you wait for me? → No, I will not wait for you.
2) Will you turn off the TV? →
3) Will you ask her out? →
4) Will you call her again? →
5) Will you do it again? →

3. will not을 사용하여 질문에 답하시오.

1) Will you go to university? →
2) Are you going to help her? →
3) Will you forget about it? →
4) Will he come back anytime soon? →
5) Will they accept my suggestion? →

4. will not과 주어진 단어를 사용하여 대화를 완성하시오.

| difficult | let down | listen | ask out | regret |

1) You betrayed me once. How can I trust you? → Trust me. I _____ you
2) What if he asks me out? What should I do? → Don't worry about it. He _____ you
3) Do you think I should take this opportunity? → Yeah, just take it. You _____ it.
4) I did not study at all for the exam. → Don't worry. It _____ .
5) Why don't you ask him again? → I gave up. He _____ to me.

5. will not을 사용하여 여러분의 다짐을 쓰시오.

1) I will not fight with my brother.
2)
3)
4)
5)
6)

UNIT 39

I can ___
저는 ___ㄹ 수 있어요/을 수 있어요

I — **can**

be - 되다
I can be a legend.
저는 전설이 될 수 있어요.

be - 지다
I can be better.
저는 더 나아질 수 있어요.
(더 잘할 수 있어요.)

do - 하다
I can handle it.
저는 그것을 다룰 수 있어요.

you — **can**

You can be a legend, too.
당신도 전설이 될 수 있어요.

You can be free.
당신은 자유로워질 수 있어요.

You can do anything.
당신은 어떤 것이든 할 수 있어요.

we — **can**

We can be a team.
우리는 같은 편이 될 수 있어요.

We can be strong.
우리는 강해질 수 있어요.

We can memorize it.
우리는 그것을 외울 수 있어요.

they — **can**

They can be classmates.
그들은 반 친구가 될 수 있어요.

They can be different.
그들은 달라질 수 있어요.

They can destroy you.
그들은 당신을 파괴할 수 있어요.

he — **can**

He can be a politician.
그는 정치인이 될 수 있어요.

He can be very strict.
그는 아주 엄격해질 수 있어요.

He can drive a truck.
그는 트럭을 운전할 수 있어요.

she — **can**

She can be the president.
그녀는 대통령이 될 수 있어요.

She can be picky sometimes.
그녀는 가끔 까다로워질 수 있어요.

She can finish it.
그녀는 끝낼 수 있어요.

it — **can**

It can be a good opportunity.
그것이 좋은 기회일 수 있어요.

It can be dangerous.
그것은 위험해질 수 있어요.

It can take a while.
그것은 시간이 좀 걸릴 수 있어요.

연습문제 — Unit 39

1. can을 사용하여 문장을 완성하시오.

1) I _____ do it.
   do: 하다
2) You _____ handle it.
   handle: 다루다
3) We _____ feel it.
   feel: 느끼다
4) She _____ order in French.
   order: 주문하다
5) I _____ explain.
   explain: 설명하다
6) He _____ beat you up.
   beat up: 두들겨 패다
7) We _____ download files.
   download: 내려받다
8) You _____ learn fast.
   learn: 배우다
9) It _____ awkward.
   awkward: 곤란/어색/불편하다

2. can 사용하여 질문에 맞게 답하시오.

1) Do you speak Spanish? →
2) Can she come to the party? →
3) Are you really going to make sandwiches? →
4) Will you help me? →
5) Do you want me to open it for you? →

3. 주어진 문장을 번역하시오.

1) 당신은 뭐든지 할 수 있어요. →
2) 그는 모든 것을 고칠 수 있어요. →
3) 그녀는 무언가를 느낄 수 있어요. →
4) 그들은 많은 것들을 할 수 있어요. →
5) 우리는 언제든지 만날 수 있어요. →

4. 주어진 단어와 can을 사용하여 문장을 완성하시오.

> (make, applications)　(make, furniture)　(ice skate)　(fix, things)　(teach, Chinese)

1) I'm a teacher and I'm from China. → I
2) Sarah is a professional hockey player. → She
3) Kevin and Amy are developers. → They
4) My dad was a carpenter. → He
5) We were engineers. → We

5. can을 사용하여 여러분, 혹은 주위 사람들이 할 수 있는 것을 쓰시오.

1)　　　　　　　　4)
2)　　　　　　　　5)
3)　　　　　　　　6)

UNIT 40

Can you ___?
___ㄹ 수 있어요?/을 수 있어요?, ___도/어도/해도 돼요?

I — I can → can I?

get
받다/사다/얻다
Can I get it?
(제가) 그것을 받아도 돼요?
→ How can I get it?
(제가) 그것을 어떻게 얻을 수 있어요?

you — you can → can you?

speak
(언어를) 하다
Can you speak Korean?
당신은 한국어를 할 수 있어요?
→ What language can you speak?
(당신은) 무슨 언어를 할 수 있어요?

we — we can → can we?

rest
쉬다
Can we rest a little bit?
우리 조금 쉬어도 돼요?
*a little = a bit = a little bit
→ How long can we rest?
(우리는) 얼마나 오래 쉴 수 있어요?

they — they can → can they?

solve
해결하다
Can they solve it?
그들이 그것을 해결할 수 있어요?
→ How can they solve it?
(그들이) 그것을 어떻게 해결할 수 있어요?

he — he can → can he?

play
(운동, 음악을) 하다
Can he play golf?
그는 골프를 칠 수 있어요?
→ Which sports can he play?
그는 어느 운동을 할 수 있어요?

she — she can → can she?

drive
운전하다
Can she drive?
그녀는 운전할 수 있어요?
→ How well can she drive?
그녀는 얼마나 잘 운전할 수 있어요?

it — it can → can it?

fly
날다
Can it fly?
그것은 날 수 있어요?
→ How far can it fly?
그것은 얼마나 멀리 날 수 있어요?

연습문제 — Unit 40

1. can을 사용하여 문장을 완성하시오.

1) _____ I borrow 4 dollars?
borrow: 빌리다
2) _____ you ask him?
ask: 물어보다
3) _____ he edit videos?
edit: 편집하다
4) _____ we just wait?
just: 그냥, 그저, 단지
5) _____ I have your number?
have: 갖다, 있다
6) _____ you forgive me?
forgive: 용서하다
7) _____ she use it?
use: 사용하다
8) _____ we talk for a second?
for a second: 잠시동안
9) _____ I order now?
order: 주문하다
10) _____ I take this?
take: 가지고 가다
11) _____ you handle it?
handle: 다루다, 감당하다
12) _____ I ask a question?
ask a question: 질문하다

2. 주어진 단어와 can을 사용하여 질문에 맞게 답하시오.

> get   help   ask a question   go for a walk   join

1) _____ → Sure. I know everything.
2) _____ → No, thanks. I'm fine.
3) _____ → I don't think they can join the party.
4) _____ → Sorry, I'm busy at the moment.
5) _____ → My phone number? What for?

3. can을 사용하여 주어진 예문에 맞는 대화를 완성하시오.

1) I lived in Germany for 10 years. → _____ speak German?
2) She rarely uses her car. → _____ drive it?
3) I have a lot of money. → _____ borrow some?
4) You don't have to hurry. Take your time. → _____ wait for me?
5) I don't use these tools anymore. → _____ have them?

4. 주어진 문장을 번역하시오.

1) 당신은 얼마나 많은 언어를 구사할 수 있어요? → _____
2) 제가 얼마를 빌릴 수 있을까요? → _____
3) 제가 당신을 위해서 무엇을 할 수 있을까요? → _____
4) 그는 무슨 종류의 동영상을 편집할 수 있어요? → _____
5) 그녀는 언제 그것을 끝낼 수 있어요? → _____

5. can을 '~해도 돼요?'의 형태로 사용하여 질문을 만드시오.

1) _____
2) _____
3) _____
4) _____
5) _____
6) _____

UNIT 41

I can not ___

못 ___ 요/어요/해요 = ___ㄹ 수 없어요/을 수 없어요

I ·· can not → can't ··

| admit | I can not admit it. | → | I can't admit the fact. |
| 인정하다 | 저는 그것을 인정할 수 없어요. | | |

you ·· can not → can't ··

| take | You can not take it. | → | You can't take my ring. |
| 가지고 가다 | 당신을 그것을 갖고 갈 수 없어요. | | |

we ·· can not → can't ··

| afford | We can not afford it. | → | We can't afford a camper. |
| 여유가 있다 | 우리는 그것을 살 수 있는 여유가 없어요. | | |

they ·· can not → can't ··

| take away | They can not take it away. | → | They can't take it away from me. |
| 빼앗아가다 | 그들은 그것을 빼앗아갈 수 없어요. | | |

he ·· can not → can't ··

| accept | He can not accept it. | → | He can't accept my apology. |
| 받아들이다 | 그는 그것을 받아들일 수 없어요. | | |

she ·· can not → can't ··

| pay | She can not pay the rent. | → | She can't pay the rent this month. |
| (돈을) 내다 | 그녀는 집세를 낼 수 없어요. | | |

it ·· can not → can't ··

| true | It can not be true. | → | The rumor can't be true. |
| 사실 | 그것이 사실일 리가 없어요. | | |

연습문제   Unit 41

1. can't를 사용하여 문장을 완성하시오.

1) I _____ afford it.
   afford: (~을 살) 여유가 있다

2) You _____ judge me.
   judge: 판단하다

3) I _____ concentrate.
   concentrate: 집중하다

4) She _____ betray me.
   betray: 배신하다

5) I _____ explain.
   explain: 설명하다

6) I _____ accept it.
   accept: 받아들이다

7) We _____ trust you anymore.
   trust: 신뢰하다

8) You _____ do that.
   do: 하다

9) It _____ real.
   real: 진짜

2. can't를 사용하여 질문에 맞게 답하시오.

1) Can you trust her? → No, _____
2) Can you explain that in English? → No, _____
3) Can I do that? → No, _____
4) Can we afford to buy a house? → No, _____
5) Can he fix it? → No, _____

3. can't를 사용하여 주어진 문장을 번역하시오.

1) 우리는 그것을 살 수 있는 여유가 없어요. → _____
2) 그것이 틀릴 수는 없어요. → _____
3) 저는 그것을 받아들일 수 없어요. → _____
4) 저는 집중할 수 없어요. → _____
5) 당신은 이렇게 나를 배신할 수 없어요. → _____

4. 주어진 단어와 can't를 사용하여 문장을 완성하시오.

> (speak, German)   (swim)   (concentrate)   (afford)   (pay)

1) I lived in Australia for a year, so I can speak a little English, but _____
2) She can swim in the ocean because she is brave, but _____ because I'm scared.
3) I have to finish my homework by 5:00 p.m, but _____ because my nephew is making noise.
4) My sister wanted to buy a dress for a party but she didn't buy it because _____
5) Can I pay the rent next month? I just lost my job, so I think _____ this month.

5. can't를 사용하여 여러분, 혹은 주위 사람들이 할 수 없는 것을 쓰시오.

1) _____
2) _____
3) _____
4) _____
5) _____
6) _____

UNIT 42

I want to ___
저는 ___고 싶어요

I — want to → wanna

be - 되다
I want to be a singer.
저는 가수가 되고 싶어요.

be - 지다
I want to be healthy.
저는 건강해지고 싶어요.

do - 하다
I want to leave.
저는 떠나고 싶어요.

---

you — want to → wanna

You want to be a farmer.
당신은 농부가 되고 싶어해요.

You want to be strong.
당신은 강해지고 싶어해요.

You want to travel.
당신은 여행하고 싶어해요.

---

we — want to → wanna

We want to be artists.
우리는 예술가가 되고 싶어요.

We want to be free.
우리는 자유로워지고 싶어요.

We want to know.
우리는 알고 싶어요.

---

they — want to → wanna

They want to be models.
그들은 모델이 되고 싶어해요.

They want to be special.
그들은 특별해지고 싶어해요.

They want to ride a bicycle.
그들은 자전거를 타고 싶어해요.

---

he — wants to

He wants to be a businessman.
그는 사업가가 되고 싶어해요.

He wants to be tall.
그는 키가 커지고 싶어해요.

He wants to go to England.
그는 영국에 가고 싶어해요.

---

she — wants to

She wants to be a painter.
그녀는 화가가 되고 싶어해요.

She wants to be pretty.
그녀는 예뻐지고 싶어해요.

She wants to live in Busan.
그녀는 부산에서 살고 싶어해요.

---

it — wants to

My dog wants to be your buddy.
저의 개는 당신의 친구가 되고 싶어해요.

My dog wants to be outside.
저의 개는 밖에 있고 싶어해요.

My dog wants to bite me.
저의 개는 저를 물고 싶어해요.

연습문제 Unit 42

1. want to를 사용하여 문장을 완성하시오.

1) I _____ leave.
leave: 떠나다

2) He _____ travel alone.
travel: 여행하다

3) They _____ challenge us.
challenge: 도전하다

4) She _____ an actress.
actress: 여배우

5) I _____ hold your hand.
hold one's hand: ~의 손을 잡다

6) I _____ free.
free: 자유롭다

7) I _____ get a haircut.
get a haircut: 머리를 깎다

8) She _____ bilingual.
bilingual: 2개 국어를 구사하다

9) He _____ figure it out.
figure out: 해결하다

10) You _____ organize a party.
organize a party: 파티를 기획하다

11) I _____ run away.
run away: 도망가다

12) She _____ ask him out.
ask him out: 그에게 데이트를 신청하다

2. 다음을 영어로 번역하시오.

1) 저는 멋져지고 싶어요. →
2) 저는 아빠가 되고 싶어요. →
3) 저는 멋진 아빠가 되고 싶어요. →
4) 그녀는 유명해지고 싶어해요. →
5) 그는 자전거를 타고 싶어해요. →

3. want to를 사용하여 질문에 답하시오.

1) Where do you want to travel? →
2) Why do you want to go there? →
3) What do you want to do there? →
4) Who do you want to meet there? →
5) When do you want to go there? →
6) Where do you want to stay? →
7) What do you want to buy there? →
8) What do you want to eat? →
9) What places do you want to visit? →
10) When do you want to come back? →

4. want to를 사용하여 내가 하고 싶은 것이나 타인이 하고 싶어 하는 것을 쓰시오.

1)
2)
3)
4)
5)
6)

UNIT 43

Do you want to ___?
___고 싶어요?

I ········· want to → wanna ·········

quit
그만두다

Do I want to quit? → Why do I want to quit?
(제가) 그만두고 싶냐고요?
(나는) 그만두고 싶은가?

---

you ········· want to → wanna ·········

know
알다

Do you want to know? → What do you want to know?
(당신은) 알고 싶으세요?

---

we ········· want to → wanna ·········

rent
대여하다

Do we want to rent a car? → How long do we want to rent a car?
우리는 차를 대여하고 싶나요?

---

they ········· want to → wanna ·········

move out
이사가다

Do they want to move out? → When do they want to move out?
그들은 이사가고 싶어해요?

---

he ········· want to → wanna ·········

move in
이사오다

Does he want to move in? → What day does he want to move in?
그는 이사오고 싶어해요?

---

she ········· want to → wanna ·········

leave
떠나다

Does she want to leave? → Why does she want to leave?
그녀는 떠나고 싶어해요?

연습문제　　　　　　　　　　　　　　　Unit 43

1. want to를 사용하여 질문을 완성하시오.

1) ____ you ____ leave now?　2) ____ he ____ play pool?　3) ____ they ____ visit us?
4) ____ she ____ build a house?　5) ____ you ____ with me?　6) ____ I ____ famous?
7) ____ he ____ change it?　8) ____ you ____ my wife?　9) ____ she ____ move in?
10) ____ you ____ move out?　11) ____ they ____ see me?　12) ____ you ____ try this?

2. want to를 사용하여 대답에 맞게 질문하시오.

1) _____ → Yes, I want to buy a car.
2) _____ → Yes, she wants to try it.
3) _____ → Yes, they want to live together.
4) _____ → Yes, he wants to live in Australia.
5) _____ → Yes, I want to be happy.

3. want to를 알맞게 사용하여 질문을 완성하시오.

1) What ____ you ____ do?　　　　6) Where ____ you ____ go?
2) Who ____ you ____ meet?　　　　7) What ____ she ____ do?
3) What film ____ you ____ watch?　8) When ____ I ____ get started?
4) What time ____ she ____ come?　9) Which one ____ he ____ take?
5) What kind of book ____ you ____ read?　10) What sort of music ____ you ____ listen to?

*kind of → kinda　　　　　　　　　　*sort of → sorta

4. when, where, who, what, how, why와 want to를 알맞게 사용하여 질문하시오.

1) _____ → I want to go to Malaysia because I speak Malay.
2) _____ → She wants to be a lawyer because she likes law.
3) _____ → They want to hang out with their cousins.
4) _____ → He wants to meet her because she is amazing.
5) _____ → They want to leave now.

5. want to를 사용하여 질문과 답변을 만드시오.

1) _____ → _____
2) _____ → _____
3) _____ → _____

UNIT 44 I don't want to ___
___고 싶지 않아요 = ___기 싫어요

I
want to → wanna

I don't want to be a failure.
저는 실패자가 되기 싫어요.

I don't want to be famous.
저는 유명해지고 싶지 않아요.

I don't want to agree.
저는 동의하고 싶지 않아요.

you
want to → wanna

You don't want to be a criminal.
당신은 범죄자가 되고 싶어하지 않아요.

You don't want to be fake.
당신은 가짜가 되고 싶지 않을 거예요.

You don't want to argue.
당신은 말싸움하기 싫어해요.

we
want to → wanna

We don't want to be liars.
우리는 거짓말쟁이들이 되고 싶지 않아요.

We don't want to be sorry.
우리는 후회하고 싶지 않아요.

We don't want to negotiate.
우리는 협상하고 싶지 않아요.

they
want to → wanna

They don't want to be rivals.
그들은 경쟁자가 되고 싶어하지 않아요.

They don't want to be ordinary.
그들은 평범해지고 싶어하지 않아요.

They don't want to punish him.
그들은 그를 처벌하고 싶어하지 않아요.

he
want to → wanna

He doesn't want to be a waiter.
그는 웨이터가 되고 싶어하지 않아요.

He doesn't want to be arrogant.
그는 거만해지고 싶어하지 않아요.

He doesn't want to betray her.
그는 그녀를 배신하고 싶어하지 않아요.

she
want to → wanna

She doesn't want to be a waitress.
그녀 웨이터가 되고 싶어하지 않아요.

She doesn't want to be picky.
그녀는 까다로워지고 싶어하지 않아요.

She doesn't want to move out.
그녀는 이사가고 싶어하지 않아요.

연습문제 Unit 44

1. don't want to를 사용하여 문장을 완성하시오.

1) I _____ talk to you.
2) She _____ a housewife.
3) I _____ worry about it.
4) You _____ my husband.
5) They _____ stop.
6) He _____ go fishing.
7) He _____ go to bed.
8) She _____ go out with him.
9) She _____ say anything.
10) I _____ make fun of you.
11) I _____ your friend.
12) We _____ popular.

2. don't want to를 사용하여 질문에 맞게 답하시오.

1) Do you want to live with me? →
2) Does she want to be with you? →
3) Do you want to work all day long? →
4) Do people want to work out on weekends? →
5) Do you want to tell me everything? →

3. want to를 사용하여 질문을 만들고 don't want to를 사용하여 답변을 하여 대화를 완성하시오.

1) →
2) →
3) →
4) →
5) →

4. don't want to를 사용하여 질문에 맞게 답하시오.

1) What movie do you want to watch? → _____ any movie.
2) Where do you want to go? → _____ anywhere.
3) What book do you want to read? → _____ any books.
4) What do you want to do today? → _____ anything.
5) Who do you want to meet tomorrow? → _____ anyone.

5. don't want to와 but, 그리고 want to를 사용하여 문장을 만드시오.

1)
2)
3)

105

UNIT 45

I want you to ___
저는 당신이 ___기를 원해요

I — I want someone to

I want **you** to be a scientist.
저는 당신이 과학자가 되기를 원해요.

I want **you** to be strong.
저는 당신이 강해지기를 원해요.

I want **you** to drive.
저는 당신이 운전하기를 원해요.

you — you want someone to

You want **me** to be an artist.
당신은 제가 예술가가 되기를 원해요.

You want **me** to be nice.
당신은 제가 착해지기를 원해요.

You want **me** to leave.
당신은 제가 떠나기를 원해요.

we — we want someone to

We want **her** to be an actress.
우리는 그녀가 여배우가 되기를 원해요.

We want **her** to be happy.
우리는 그녀가 행복해지기를 원해요.

We want **her** to come back.
우리는 그녀가 돌아오기를 원해요.

they — they want someone to

They want **him** to be an actor.
그들은 그가 배우가 되기를 원해요.

They want **him** to be lonely.
그들은 그가 외로워지기를 원해요.

They want **him** to go back.
그들은 그가 돌아가기를 원해요.

he — he wants someone to

He want**s** **them** to be friends.
그는 그들이 친구가 되기를 원해요.

He wants **them** to be healthy.
그는 그들이 건강해지기를 원해요.

He wants **them** to wait.
그는 그들이 기다리기를 원해요.

she — she wants someone to

She want**s** **us** to be colleagues.
그녀는 우리가 동료가 되기를 원해요.

She wants **us** to be different.
그녀는 우리가 달라지기를 원해요.

She wants **us** to stay.
그녀는 우리가 머무르기를 원해요.

연습문제　　　　　　　　　　　　　　　Unit 45

1. want someone to를 사용하여 문장을 완성하시오.

1) I ____ you ____ leave now.
2) She ____ him ____ nice.
3) I ____ you ____ help me.
4) They ____ us ____ come back.
5) She ____ you ____ better.
6) He ____ me ____ remember.
7) He ____ her ____ different.
8) We ____ them ____ safe.
9) Tom ____ David ____ run away.
10) They ____ you ____ get up.
11) My parents ____ him ____ stay.
12) She ____ you ____ a model.

2. want someone to를 사용하여 문장을 완성하시오.

1) I ____ you ____ leave me alone.
2) They ____ him ____ get up early.
3) I ____ you ____ wake her up.
4) She ____ me ____ a good person.
5) I ____ them ____ forget everything.
6) I ____ you ____ buy me something.
7) He ____ them ____ work hard.
8) We ____ them ____ have fun.
9) She ____ me ____ pay her back.
10) They ____ her ____ work out.
11) He ____ me ____ call her.
12) She ____ Kevin ____ stay longer.

3. want someone to를 사용하여 문장을 완성하시오.

1) He ____ you ____ pay him back.
2) She ____ him ____ clean the house.
3) He ____ me ____ drive his car.
4) We ____ her ____ take the job.
5) I ____ her ____ hold my hand.
6) I ____ them ____ stay in my place.
7) I ____ you ____ take care of my son.
8) They ____ her ____ have fun .
9) She ____ them ____ bring Jane's cup.
10) They ____ us ____ rest more.
11) We ____ them ____ enjoy it.
12) I ____ you ____ take my jacket.

4. want someone to를 사용하여 주어진 질문에 답하시오.

1) What do you want your dad to do?　　1) ____
2) What does your mom want you to do?　　2) ____
3) How long do you want your cousin to stay?　　3) ____
4) Where do you want your friend to take you to?　　4) ____
5) What kind of people do your parents want you to hang out with?　　5) ____

UNIT 46 Do you want me to ___?
당신은 제가 ___기를 원해요?

me ──────── do you want me to ────────

Do you want me to disappear? → Why do you want me to disappear?
당신은 제가 사라지기를 원해요?

you ──────── do they want you to ────────

Do they want you to work? → When do they want you to work?
그들은 당신이 일하기를 원해요?

us ──────── do you want us to ────────

Do you want us to stay? → How long do you want us to stay?
당신은 우리가 머무르기를 원해요?

them ──────── do you want them to ────────

Do you want them to come? → When do you want them to come?
당신은 그들이 오기를 원해요?

him ──────── do you want him to ────────

Do you want him to have it? → Why do you want him to have it?
당신은 그가 그것을 갖기를 원해요?

her ──────── do you want her to ────────

Does he want her to come back? → When does he want her to come back?
그는 그녀가 돌아오기를 원해요?

it ──────── do you want it to ────────

Do you want it to be special? → Why do you want it to be special?
당신은 그것이 특별하기를 원해요?

연습문제 — Unit 46

1. want someone to와 [ ]의 단어를 순서대로 사용하여 질문을 완성하시오.

1) [you, me]　　Do you want me to settle?
2) [they, him]　　_____ answer?
3) [you, me]　　_____ normal?
4) [he, me]　　_____ an expert?
5) [he, her]　　_____ a model?
6) [she, you]　　_____ go back?
7) [Jenny, them]　　_____ quiet?
8) [I, her]　　_____ popular?
9) [you, me]　　_____ your husband?
10) [why, you, me]　　_____ wait?

2. want someone to를 사용하여 대화를 완성하시오.

1) _____? Yes, I want you to stay here.
2) _____? Yes, I want him to stay away from her.
3) _____? Yes, he wants me to take it.
4) _____? Yes, they want her to take care of it.
5) _____? Yes, she wants them to have fun.
6) _____? Yes, I want you to get better.

3. when, where, who, what, how 등과 want someone to를 사용하여 대화를 완성하시오.

(how long, stay)　(at what time, there)　(where, take)　(what, do)　(when, come)

1) _____? I want you to take me to the beach.
2) _____? I want them to stay here for a week.
3) _____? He wants you guys to be there on time.
4) _____? I want you to stay out of my life.
5) _____? They want her to come next Tuesday.

4. want someone to를 사용하여 질문을 만드시오.

1)
2)
3)
4)
5)

UNIT 47 I don't want you to ___
저는 당신이 ___는 것을 원하지 않아요

I ············ I don't want someone to ············

Do you want me to help? → I don't want you to help.
저는 당신이 돕는 것을 원하지 않아요.

you ············ you don't want someone to ············

Do I want you to cook? → You don't want me to cook.
당신은 제가 요리하는 것을 원하지 않아요.

we ············ we don't want someone to ············

Do you guys want us to wait? → We don't want you guys to wait.
우리는 당신들이 기다리는 것을 원하지 않아요

they ············ they don't want someone to ············

Do they want him to fail? → They don't want him to fail.
그들은 그가 실패하는 것을 원하지 않아요.

he ············ he doesn't want someone to ············

Does he want her to leave? → He doesn't want her to leave.
그는 그녀가 떠나는 것을 원하지 않아요.

she ············ she doesn't want someone to ············

Does she want them to come? → She doesn't want them to come.
그녀는 그들이 오는 것을 원하지 않아요.

연습문제　　　　　　　　　　　　　　　　Unit 47

1. don't want someone to를 사용하여 문장을 완성하시오.

1) I _____ you _____ a liar.
liar: 거짓말쟁이

2) They _____ her _____ a failure.
failure: 실패자

3) She _____ her son _____ an employee.
employee: 종업원

4) You _____ him _____ a landlord.
landlord: 집주인

5) She _____ him _____ a criminal.
criminal: 범죄자

6) We _____ you _____ a winner.
winner: 승리자

7) He _____ his daughter _____ an actress.
actress: 여배우

8) My dad _____ me _____ a tenant.
tenant: 세입자

2. don't want someone/something to를 사용하여 문장을 완성하시오.

1) We _____ you _____ lonely.
lonely: 외롭다

2) I _____ her _____ famous.
famous: 유명하다

3) Our parents _____ us _____ selfish.
selfish: 이기적이다

4) I _____ you _____ pessimistic.
pessimistic: 비관적이다

5) I _____ him _____ lazy.
lazy: 게으르다

6) We _____ the test _____ difficult.
difficult: 어렵다

7) She _____ them _____ greedy.
greedy: 탐욕스럽다

8) My husband _____ me _____ optimistic.
optimistic: 낙관적이다

3. don't want someone to를 사용하여 문장을 완성하시오.

1) We _____ you _____ get hurt.
get hurt: 다치다

2) I _____ you _____ put it down.
put down: 내려놓다

3) You _____ me _____ press the button.
press: 누르다

4) I _____ him _____ break my heart.
break one's heart: ~의 마음을 무너뜨리다

5) She _____ me _____ keep it.
keep: 유지하다, 보관하다

6) I _____ you _____ hold her hand.
hold: 잡다

7) They _____ us _____ kick him out.
kick out: 내쫓다

8) We _____ them _____ bring it back.
bring back: 다시 가지고 오다

4. don't want someone to를 사용하여 대화를 완성하시오.

1) Do you want me to take care of her?　　No, _____ take care of her.

2) Does she want him to be jealous?　　No, _____ jealous.

3) Do they want me to join?　　No, _____ join.

4) Does he want her to be his girlfriend?　　No, _____ his girlfriend.

5) Do you want them to understand?　　No, _____ understand.

6) Do they want us to be popular?　　No, _____ popular.

7) Do you want me to be alone?　　No, _____ alone.

UNIT 48

I need to ___
저는 ___ ㄹ 필요가 있어요/을 필요가 있어요

I ———————————— need to ————————————

I need to be honest.
저는 정직할 필요가 있어요.

I need to get a girlfriend.
저는 여자친구를 만들 필요가 있어요.

you ———————————— need to ————————————

You need to be brave.
당신은 용감할 필요가 있어요.

You need to calm down.
당신은 진정할 필요가 있어요.

we ———————————— need to ————————————

We need to be patient.
우리는 참을 필요가 있어요.

We need to keep the secret.
우리는 비밀을 지킬 필요가 있어요.

they ———————————— need to ————————————

They need to be easy.
그것들은 쉬울 필요가 있어요.

They need to challenge him.
그들은 그에게 도전할 필요가 있어요.

he ———————————— needs to ————————————

He needs to be creative.
그는 창의적일 필요가 있어요.

He needs to wear glasses.
그는 안경을 쓸 필요가 있어요.

she ———————————— needs to ————————————

She needs to be generous.
그녀는 관대할 필요가 있어요.

She needs to rest.
그녀는 쉴 필요가 있어요.

it ———————————— needs to ————————————

It needs to be fair.
그것은 공평할 필요가 있어요.

It needs to stop.
그것은 중단될 필요가 있어요.

연습문제　　　　　　　　　　　　　　　　　　　　　Unit 48

1. need to를 사용하여 문장을 완성하시오.

1) You _____ accept it.
   accept: 받아들이다

2) I _____ there for her.
   be there: 그곳에 있다

3) We _____ submit a document.
   submit a document: 서류를 제출하다

4) I _____ go on a diet.
   go on a diet: 다이어트를 하다

5) I _____ get a new job.
   get: 얻다

6) He _____ get away from here.
   get away: 벗어나다

7) She _____ calm down.
   calm down: 진정하다

8) We _____ escape from here.
   escape: 탈출하다

9) They _____ creative.
   creative: 창의적이다

2. 주어진 단어와 need to를 알맞게 사용하여 대화를 완성하시오.

> practice　　finish　　eat　　work　　save up

1) I want to speak German fluently. → Well, then you _____ every day.
2) I want to travel all over the world. → Then, you _____ a lot of money.
3) She wants to get a full time job. → Then she _____ hard.
4) He doesn't want to be sick. → Well, then he _____ healthy food.
5) Do you have to do it now? → Yes, because I _____ this by tomorrow.

3. 주어진 단어와 need to를 알맞게 사용하여 문장을 완성하시오.

1) (stay up all night) → I have a lot of work, so I _____
2) (business partners) → I have a good idea, so we _____
3) (get away from everything) → I'm so stressed out. I think _____
4) (polite) → My boyfriend was so rude to my friends. He _____
5) (go on a diet) → I think they got fat. They _____

4. need to를 사용하여 해야 할 필요가 있는 일을 쓰시오.

1) _____　　6) _____
2) _____　　7) _____
3) _____　　8) _____
4) _____　　9) _____
5) _____　　10) _____

UNIT 49

Do I need to ___?
제가 ___ ㄹ필요가 있어요/을 필요가 있어요?

I — do I need to

Do I need to bow? → When do I need to bow?
제가 고개를 숙일 필요가 있어요?

you — do you need to

Do you need to marry? → Why do you need to marry?
당신은 결혼할 필요가 있어요?

we — do we need to

Do we need to have a baby? → How many babies do we need to have?
우리는 아이를 낳을 필요가 있어요?

they — do they need to

Do they need to attend? → What event do they need to attend?
그들은 참석할 필요가 있어요?

he — does he need to

Does he need to go? → How far does he need to go?
그가 갈 필요가 있어요?

she — does she need to

Does she need to take medicine? → How much medicine does she need to take?
그녀는 약을 먹을 필요가 있어요?

it — does It need to

Does it need to cool down? → How much does it need to cool down?
그것을 (차갑게) 식힐 필요가 있어요?

연습문제 — Unit 49

1. need to를 사용하여 질문을 완성하시오.

1) _____ we _____ bow?
   bow: 고개를 숙이다, 절하다
2) _____ we _____ bring them all?
   bring: 가지고 오다
3) _____ I _____ print it out?
   print out: 인쇄하다
4) _____ we _____ go to university?
   go: 가다, 다니다
5) _____ we _____ own a house?
   own: 소유하다
6) _____ you really _____ wear a scarf?
   wear: 입다
7) _____ I _____ tip in Australia?
   tip: 팁을 주다
8) _____ you _____ spend money on it?
   spend: 소비하다
9) _____ we _____ take responsibility?
   take responsibility: 책임을 지다
10) _____ I _____ register?
    register: 등록하다

2. need to를 사용하여 대화를 완성하시오.

> take a break   polite   get out   buy   tell

1) _____ ? → Of course, I need it.
2) _____ ? → Yes, I'm so tired because I stayed up all night.
3) _____ ? → Definitely. You should tell her everything.
4) _____ ? → Yes, I want you to leave now.
5) _____ ? → Absolutely! We should respect them.

3. 주어진 단어와 need to를 사용하여 대답에 맞게 질문하시오.

> (what, do) (where, get off) (at what time, get to the airport) (when, go to bed) (who, see)

1) _____ → I have no idea.
2) _____ → You should see a doctor.
3) _____ → Probably sooner or later.
4) _____ → I should get there around 3p.m.
5) _____ → We need to get off at the next station.

4. 주어진 문장을 읽고 need to를 사용하여 질문하시오.

1) I need to meet her.   → Why _____
2) I need to leave soon. → At what time exactly _____
3) We need to wait.   → How long _____
4) They need to pay.   → How much _____
5) She needs to walk.   → How far _____

UNIT 50 I don't need to ___
저는 ___ㄹ 필요가 없어요/을 필요가 없어요

I ·· don't need to ··

I don't need to be a cook.
저는 요리사가 될 필요가 없어요.

I don't need to be polite.
저는 공손할 필요가 없어요.

I don't need to compete.
저는 경쟁할 필요가 없어요.

you ·· don't need to ··

You don't need to be a jerk.
당신은 얼간이가 될 필요가 없어요.

You don't need to be brave.
당신은 용감할 필요가 없어요.

You don't need to choose.
당신은 선택할 필요가 없어요.

we ·· don't need to ··

We don't need to be partners.
우리는 파트너가 될 필요가 없어요.

We don't need to be patient.
우리는 참을 필요가 없어요.

We don't need to tip.
우리는 팁을 줄 필요가 없어요.

they ·· don't need to ··

They don't need to be roommates.
그들은 룸메이트가 될 필요가 없어요.

They don't need to be bright.
그것들은 밝을 필요가 없어요.

They don't need to share it.
그들은 그것을 공유할 필요가 없어요.

he ·· doesn't need to ··

He doesn't need to be an expert.
그는 전문가가 될 필요가 없어요.

He doesn't need to be creative.
그는 창의적일 필요가 없어요.

He doesn't need to fight.
그는 싸울 필요가 없어요.

she ·· doesn't need to ··

She doesn't need to be a model.
그녀는 모델이 될 필요가 없어요.

She doesn't need to be mad.
그녀는 화를 낼 필요가 없어요.

She doesn't need to agree.
그녀는 동의할 필요가 없어요.

it ·· doesn't need to ··

It doesn't need to be right now.
그것은 지금 당장이 될 필요는 없어요.

It doesn't need to be fresh.
그것은 신선할 필요가 없어요.

It doesn't need to start yet.
그것은 아직 시작할 필요가 없어요.

연습문제 — Unit 50

1. don't need to를 사용하여 질문을 완성하시오.

1) You _____ remove it.
2) I _____ go all the way up.
3) He _____ press the button.
4) It _____ similar.
5) We _____ share everything.
6) You _____ tip in Asian countries.
7) We _____ write it down.
8) She _____ serious about it.

2. don't need to를 사용하여 질문에 맞게 답하시오.

1) Do you need to have a tutor? → No, _____
2) Do we need to graduate from university? → No, _____
3) Do I need to go all the way downstairs? → No, _____
4) Does it need to be similar to this? → No, _____
5) Do I need to have a degree? → No, _____

3. do you need to와 don't need to를 사용하여 질문과 답변을 완성하시오.

1) _____ → _____
2) _____ → _____
3) _____ → _____
4) _____ → _____
5) _____ → _____

4. don't need to를 사용하여 문장을 완성하시오.

1) Do I have to tell you everything? → No, _____
2) Should I explain it again? → No, _____
3) I don't want to live in the city. → _____
4) I can't do it right now. → _____
5) Why should I tip? → _____

5. don't need to와 because를 사용하여 문장을 만드시오.

1) _____
2) _____
3) _____
4) _____
5) _____

UNIT 51

I have to ___
저는 ___야 해요/어야 해요/해야 해요

I have got to → I've got to → I've gotta → I gotta

I
have to → gotta

I **have to be** a winner.
저는 승자가 되어야 해요.

I **have to be** modest.
저는 겸손해야 해요.

I **have to** write it down.
저는 그것을 받아 적어야 해요.

you
have to → gotta

You have to be a dancer.
당신은 댄서가 되어야 해요.

You have to be confident.
당신은 자신감을 가져야 해요.

You have to check it out.
당신은 그것을 확인해야 해요.

we
have to → gotta

We have to be free men.
우리는 자유인이 되어야 해요.

We have to be generous.
우리는 관대해야 해요.

We have to pack.
우리는 짐을 싸야 해요.

they
have to → gotta

They have to be a team.
그들은 한 팀이 되어야 해요.

They have to be quiet.
그들은 조용해야 해요.

They have to unpack.
그들은 짐을 풀어야 해요.

he
he has to → he's gotta

He has to be a problem solver.
그는 해결사가 되어야 해요.

He has to be serious.
그는 진지해야 해요.

He has to reply.
그는 답장해야 해요.

she
she has to → she's gotta

She has to be a pianist.
그녀는 피아니스트가 되어야 해요.

She has to be outgoing.
그녀는 외향적이어야 해요.

She has to apply.
그녀는 지원해야 해요.

it
it has to → it's gotta

It has to be an answer.
그것은 정답이어야 해요.

It has to be correct.
그것은 맞아야 해요.

It has to stop.
그것은 멈춰야 해요.

연습문제　　　　　　　　　　　　　　　　Unit 51

1. have to를 사용하여 문장을 완성하시오.

1) I _____ figure it out.　2) You _____ answer.　3) We _____ apply.

4) They _____ check this out.　5) He _____ modest.　6) She _____ reply.

7) It _____ simple.　8) I _____ make her happy.　9) You _____ confident.

2. have to와 주어진 단어를 사용하여 질문에 맞게 답하시오.

> figure it out　　work　　confident　　go　　call

1) Do you want to hang out with us today?　→ No, I don't have time because I _____

2) Are you going to call her?　→ Yeah. I think I _____

3) I'm not confident at all.　→ What? Why? You _____

4) I don't want to go there.　→ But you _____

5) I think I have to figure it out.　→ Yes, you _____

3. have to를 사용하여 질문에 맞게 답하시오.

1) What are you going to do tomorrow?　→ _____

2) What time do you have to leave?　→ _____

3) What do you want to do next weekend?　→ _____

4) Where do you have to go today?　→ _____

5) Why do you study?　→ _____

4. have to를 사용하여 오늘과 내일 해야 할 것들을 작성하시오.

1) _____　　6) _____
2) _____　　7) _____
3) _____　　8) _____
4) _____　　9) _____
5) _____　　10) _____

UNIT 52 Do I have to ___?
제가 ___야 해요/어야 해요/해야 해요?

I — do I have to

Do I have to do it?
제가 그것을 해야 해요?
→ Why do I have to do it?

you — do you have to

Do you have to work?
당신은 일을 해야 해요?
→ What day do you have to work?

we — do we have to

Do we have to apologize?
우리가 사과해야 해요?
→ How many times do we have to apologize?

they — do they have to

Do they have to get a job?
그들은 직업을 가져야 해요?
→ What kind of job do they have to get?
*what kind of: 무슨 종류의 kind of → kinda

he — does he have to

Does he have to pay?
그가 돈을 내야 해요?
→ How much does he have to pay?

she — does she have to

Does she have to save up?
그녀가 돈을 모아야 해요?
→ How much does she have to save up?

it — does It have to

Does it have to be new?
그것이 새것이어야 해요?
→ Why does it have to be new?

연습문제 — Unit 52

1. have to를 사용하여 질문을 완성하시오.

1) _____ I _____ answer now?
2) _____ we _____ buy them all?
3) _____ she _____ pass an exam?
4) _____ you _____ leave me?
5) _____ I _____ figure it out?
6) _____ he _____ work all day long?

2. have to를 사용하여 대답에 맞는 질문을 완성하시오.

1) _____ → Yes, I have to do it.
2) _____ → Yes, you have to come.
3) _____ → Yes, we have to figure it out.
4) _____ → Yes, they have to be honest.
5) _____ → Yes, I have to get a job.

3. have to를 사용하여 질문을 완성하시오.

1) Why _____ we _____ trust him?
2) What _____ I _____ do?
3) Why _____ they _____ take an exam?
4) Where _____ I _____ go?
5) Why _____ we _____ get a job?
6) How long _____ I _____ wait?

4. 주어진 단어와 have to를 사용하여 질문하시오.

((what sort of, get)   (where, get off)   (at what time, get up)   (why, leave)   (what, do))

1) _____ → Because I'm drunk.
2) _____ → We have to get off at the next station.
3) _____ → I have to get up at 7 in the morning.
4) _____ → I think you should get a leather jacket.
5) _____ → I think he has to apologize to her.

UNIT 53   I don't have to ___
안 ___도/어도/해도 돼요 = ___지 않아도 돼요

I — don't have to

I don't have to be a farmer.
저는 농부가 되지 않아도 돼요.

I don't have to be rich.
저는 부유하지 않아도 돼요.

I don't have to memorize it.
저는 그것을 외우지 않아도 돼요.

you — don't have to

You don't have to be a liar.
당신은 거짓말쟁이가 되지 않아도 돼요.

You don't have to be afraid.
당신은 두려워하지 않아도 돼요.

You don't have to worry.
당신은 걱정하지 않아도 돼요.

we — don't have to

We don't have to be enemies.
우리는 적이 되지 않아도 돼요.

We don't have to be normal.
우리는 평범하지 않아도 돼요.

We don't have to settle.
우리는 정착하지 않아도 돼요.

they — don't have to

They don't have to be a team.
그들은 한 팀이 되지 않아도 돼요.

They don't have to be serious.
그들은 심각해하지 않아도 돼요.

They don't have to run.
그들은 뛰지 않아도 돼요.

he — doesn't have to

He doesn't have to be a poet.
그는 시인이 되지 않아도 돼요.

He doesn't have to be nervous.
그는 긴장하지 않아도 돼요.

He doesn't have to choose now.
그는 지금 선택하지 않아도 돼요.

she — doesn't have to

She doesn't have to be a composer.
그녀는 작곡가가 되지 않아도 돼요.

She doesn't have to be jealous.
그녀는 질투하지 않아도 돼요.

She doesn't have to cancel.
그녀는 취소하지 않아도 돼요.

it — doesn't have to

It doesn't have to be today.
오늘이 아니어도 돼요.

It doesn't have to be great.
그것은 대단하지 않아도 돼요.

It doesn't have to make sense.
그것은 말이 되지 않아도 돼요.

연습문제　　　　　　　　　　　　　　　　　　　Unit 53

1. don't have to를 사용하여 문장을 완성하시오.

1) It _____ perfect.

2) You _____ get up early.

3) You _____ work out every day.

4) You _____ answer the phone.

5) You _____ worry about it.

6) We _____ split the bill.

7) I _____ go to work today.

8) She _____ join the military service.

2. don't have to를 사용하여 질문에 맞게 답하시오.

1) Do I have to decide now?　　→　No, _____

2) Do you have to move out?　　→　No, _____

3) Do we have to do this?　　→　No, _____

4) Does it have to be perfect?　　→　No, _____

5) Do I have to be quiet here?　　→　No, _____

3. don't have to를 사용하여 질문에 맞게 답하시오.

1) Why do you have to work all day long?　→　_____

2) What kind of clothes do we have to buy?　→　_____

3) How many times do I have to tell you?　→　_____

4) When do you have to finish it?　→　_____

5) What day do you have to leave?　→　_____

4. don't have to를 사용하여 하지 않아도 될 일을 쓰시오.

1) _____

2) _____

3) _____

4) _____

5) _____

6) _____

7) _____

8) _____

9) _____

10) _____

UNIT 54

I should ___
저는 ___야/어야/해야만 해요

I — should

I should be an athlete.
저는 운동선수가 되어야만 해요.

I should be brave.
저는 용감해야만 해요.

I should memorize it.
저는 그것을 외워야만 해요.

you — should

You should be a firefighter.
당신은 소방관이 되어야만 해요.

You should be strong.
당신은 강해야만 해요.

You should protect her.
당신은 그녀를 보호해야만 해요.

we — should

We should be vegetarians.
우리는 채식주의자가 되어야만 해요.

We should be healthy.
우리는 건강해야만 해요.

We should get off here.
우리는 여기에서 내려야만 해요.

they — should

They should be partners.
그들은 동업자가 되어야만 해요.

They should be safe.
그것들은 안전해야만 해요.

They should take the subway.
그들은 전철을 타야만 해요.

he — should

He should be my husband.
그는 제 남편이 되어야만 해요.

He should be wise.
그는 현명해야만 해요.

He should call me.
그는 저한테 전화해야만 해요.

she — should

She should be my wife.
그녀는 제 아내가 되어야만 해요.

She should be quiet.
그녀는 조용해야만 해요.

She should finish it.
그녀는 그것을 끝내야만 해요.

it — should

It should be 2 dollars.
그것은 2달러여야만 해요.

It should be easy.
그것은 쉬워야만 해요.

It should work.
그것은 작동해야만 해요.

124

연습문제　　　　　　　　　　　　　　Unit 54

1. should를 사용하여 문장을 완성하시오.

1) We _____ vegetarians.　2) I _____ there by 3:00.　3) We _____ partners.

4) We _____ healthy.　5) You _____ nice to her.　6) He _____ gentle.

7) I _____ finish it by today.　8) We _____ realize the fact.　9) They _____ recognize me.

2. 주어진 단어와 should를 알맞게 사용하여 대화를 완성하시오.

　　　　　singer　　successful　　chef　　healthy　　smart

1) I want to be an athlete.　　　　→ Then, you _____
2) She really likes to sing.　　　　→ I think she _____
3) He's really good at cooking.　　→ Well, then he _____
4) I'm going to be a teacher.　　　→ Then, you _____
5) He wants to buy a fancy car.　　→ Then, the business _____

3. 주어진 단어와 should를 알맞게 사용하여 문장을 완성하시오.

1) (go to bed, now)　　　　　　　　　→ I stayed up all night, so I _____
2) (make it work)　　　　　　　　　　→ My boss asked me to make it work, so I _____
3) (nice to my mom)　　　　　　　　 → I'm not a good son, so I _____
4) (get to, the airport, by 2:00)　　　→ My flight is 4:00, so I _____
5) (get away, from, here, immediately) → I'm so stressed out, so I _____

4. should를 사용하여 질문에 맞게 답하시오.

1) What are you going to do today?　　　　　　→
2) Where are you going this weekend?　　　　 →
3) When are you going to finish your homework? →
4) Who are you going to meet tomorrow?　　　 →
5) At what time are you going to leave?　　　　→

5. I think/I don't think와 should를 사용하여 작문하시오. *I think I should ___. = ___해야만 할 것 같다

1)
2)
3)
4)
5)

UNIT 55

Should I ___?
제가 ___야/어야/해야만 해요?

I ----------------- should I -----------------

Should I do it? → Why should I do it?
제가 그것을 해야만 해요?

you ----------------- should you -----------------

Should you take pills? → How many pills should you take?
당신은 약을 먹어야만 해요?

we ----------------- should we -----------------

Should we get off here? → Where should we get off?
우리는 여기에서 내려야만 해요?

they ----------------- should they -----------------

Should they do it? → What should they do?
그들이 그것을 해야만 해요?

he ----------------- should he -----------------

Should he apologize? → How should he apologize?
그가 사과를 해야만 해요?

she ----------------- should she -----------------

Should she ask me out? → When should she ask me out?
그녀가 저에게 데이트신청을 해야만 해요?

it ----------------- should It -----------------

Should it matter? → Why should it matter?
그것이 문제여야만 해요? (그게 중요해요?)

연습문제 — Unit 55

1. should를 사용하여 문장을 완성하시오.

1) _____ I say something?   2) _____ I ask her out?   3) _____ we go now?

4) _____ we get off here?   5) _____ I wear a mask?   6) _____ we donate money?

7) _____ I text him first?   8) _____ I apologize first?   9) _____ they kick him out?

2. should와 괄호안의 단어를 사용하여 질문을 완성하시오.

1) Where _____ ?   2) What _____ ?   3) Why _____ ?
   (we, meet)   (I, do)   (I, care)

4) Where _____ ?   5) Why _____ ?   6) Why _____ ?
   (we, get off)   (I, wear a mask)   (I, apologize)

7) What _____ ?   8) By when _____ ?   9) At what time _____ ?
   (I, say)   (I, fix this)   (we, leave)

3. 주어진 단어와 when, where, who, what, how, why, 그리고 should를 사용하여 질문하시오.

(I, finish)   (we, get off)   (I, do)   (we, meet)   (we, hire)

1) _____ → You should hire me because I'm a hard working person.
2) _____ → I think you should finish it by tonight.
3) _____ → We should get off soon.
4) _____ → You should just wait.
5) _____ → I will see you at the library.

4. should를 사용하여 질문을 만들어 대화를 완성하시오.

1) _____ → _____
2) _____ → _____
3) _____ → _____
4) _____ → _____
5) _____ → _____

5. do you think와 should를 사용하여 작문하시오. *Do you think I should ___? (___해야만 할 것 같나요?)*

1) _____
2) _____
3) _____
4) _____
5) _____

UNIT 56

I should not ___
___면/으면 안 돼요 = ___해서는 안 되다

I -------- should not → shouldn't --------

I should not be a coward.
저는 겁쟁이가 되면 안 돼요.

I should not be weak.
저는 약하면 안 돼요.

I should not mention it.
저는 그것을 언급하면 안 돼요.

you -------- should not → shouldn't --------

You should not be a scammer.
당신은 사기꾼이 되면 안 돼요.

You should not be loud.
당신은 시끄러우면 안 돼요.

You should not give up.
당신은 포기하면 안 돼요.

we -------- should not → shouldn't --------

We should not be friends.
우리는 친구가 되면 안 돼요.

We should not be greedy.
우리는 욕심을 부리면 안 돼요.

We should not curse.
우리는 욕을 하면 안 돼요.

they -------- should not → shouldn't --------

They should not be competitors.
그들은 경쟁자가 되면 안 돼요.

They should not be selfish.
그것들은 이기적이면 안 돼요.

They should not spit.
그들은 침을 뱉으면 안 돼요.

he -------- should not → shouldn't --------

He should not be my stepbrother.
그가 제 이복(남)형제가 되면 안 돼요.

He should not be picky.
그는 까다로우면 안 돼요.

He should not laugh out loud.
그는 크게 웃으면 안 돼요.

she -------- should not → shouldn't --------

She should not be my stepsister.
그녀가 제 이복(여)형제가 되면 안 돼요.

She should not be arrogant.
그녀는 거만하면 안 돼요.

She should not think too much.
그녀는 너무 많이 생각하면 안 돼요.

it -------- should not → shouldn't --------

It should not be a problem.
그것은 문제가 되면 안 돼요.

It should not be wrong.
그것은 틀리면 안 돼요.

It should not stop.
그것은 멈추면 안 돼요.

연습문제　　　　　　　　　　　　　　　　　　　Unit 56

1. shouldn't를 사용하여 문장을 완성하시오.

1) You _____ a fraud.　2) We _____ competitors.　3) She _____ my fiancé.

4) They _____ a couple.　5) He _____ my boss.　6) It _____ a joke.

7) I _____ a troublemaker. 8) You _____ a coward.　9) He _____ my stepbrother.

2. shouldn't를 사용하여 문장을 완성하시오.

1) I _____ bald.　　　　　2) It _____ itchy.　　　　3) It _____ funny.
bald: 머리가 벗겨지다　　　itchy: 가렵다　　　　　　funny: 웃기다

4) You _____ too late.　　5) You _____ pessimistic.　6) It _____ painful.
late: 늦다　　　　　　　　pessimistic: 비관적이다　　painful: 고통스럽다

7) They _____ here.　　　8) We _____ together.　　9) He _____ angry.
here: 여기　　　　　　　　together: 함께　　　　　　angry: 화가 나다, 화를 내다

3. shouldn't를 사용하여 문장을 완성하시오.

1) You _____ laugh out loud. 2) We _____ force them.　3) You _____ give up.
laugh out loud: 큰 소리를 내며 웃다　force: 강요하다　　　give up: 포기하다

4) We _____ smoke here.　5) You _____ forget.　　　6) We _____ waste resources.
smoke: 담배를 피우다　　　forget: 잊다　　　　　　　waste resources: 자원을 낭비하다

7) He _____ mention it.　8) You _____ think too much. 9) People _____ curse here.
mention: 언급하다　　　　think: 생각하다　　　　　　curse: 욕하다

4. should't를 사용하여 질문에 맞게 답하시오.

1) Should we get off here?　　　→　No, _____
2) Should I give up now?　　　　→　No, _____
3) Should I just do it?　　　　　→　No, _____
4) Should the exam be difficult?　→　No, _____
5) Should we be together?　　　→　No, _____

5. should와 shouldn't를 사용하여 대화를 완성하시오.

1) _____　→　_____
2) _____　→　_____
3) _____　→　_____
4) _____　→　_____
5) _____　→　_____

UNIT 57　I must ___

분명 ___일 거예요, ___하시겠어요, 반드시 ___해야 하다

I ———— must ————

I must be a hero.
저는 반드시 영웅이 되어야 해요.

I must be strong.
저는 반드시 강해져야 해요.

I must finish it.
저는 그것을 반드시 끝내야 해요.

you ———— must ————

You must be Jason.
당신이 바로 제이슨 씨군요.

You must be proud of him.
그가 자랑스러우시겠어요.

You must come back.
당신은 반드시 돌아와야 해요.

we ———— must ————

We must be friends.
우리는 반드시 친구가 되어야 해요.

We must be humble.
우리는 반드시 겸손해야 해요.

We must remember.
우리는 반드시 기억해야 해요.

they ———— must ————

They must be brothers.
그들은 틀림없이 형제일 거예요.

They must be kind.
그것들은 반드시 친절해야 해요.

They must apologize.
그들은 반드시 사과해야 해요.

he ———— must ————

He must be your dad.
그는 분명 당신의 아빠일 거예요.

He must be gentle.
그는 반드시 신사적이어야 해요.

He must win.
그는 반드시 이겨야 해요.

she ———— must ————

She must be single.
그녀는 분명히 미혼일 거예요.

She must be nice.
그녀는 반드시 착해야 해요.

She must calm down.
그녀는 반드시 진정해야 해요.

it ———— must ————

It must be a scam.
그것은 반드시 사기일 거예요.

It must be simple.
그것은 반드시 간단해야 해요.

It must stop.
그것은 반드시 멈춰야 해요.

연습문제 Unit 57

1. must를 사용하여 문장을 완성하시오.

1) You _____ his girlfriend. 2) He _____ a movie star. 3) She _____ a model.

4) We _____ polite. 5) You _____ quiet. 6) It _____ hard.

7) I _____ visit my parents. 8) We _____ protect them. 9) They _____ know this.

2. 주어진 단어와 must를 알맞게 사용하여 대화를 완성하시오. (틀림없이 ~일 것이다)

gift   teenager   Allison   European   thief

1) She has blonde hair. → She _____
2) He looks young. → He _____
3) Hi, nice to finally meet you. → You _____
4) What's this box? → I have no idea. Just open it. It _____
5) Who do you think the thief is? → She _____

3. 주어진 단어와 must를 알맞게 사용하여 대화를 완성하시오.

hungry   stressed   tired   busy   hard

1) I had a nightmare. I barely slept last night. → You _____
2) I will take the bar exam. → It _____
3) I haven't had anything. → You _____
4) I have studied 12 hours straight. → You _____
5) You _____ → No, not at all. I'm free as a bird.

4. 주어진 단어와 must를 알맞게 사용하여 대화를 완성하시오.

take   get   finish   call 911   apologize

1) I yelled at my mom this morning. → You _____ to your mom.
2) It's an emergency! Jack fell from a tree. → You _____
3) Let's go out tonight. → No, I can't. I _____ this by tonight.
4) Your phone is ringing. → I'm sorry, I _____ this.
5) At what time are you going to leave? → I _____ home before midnight.

UNIT 58

(1) I have ___
___한 적이 있다, ___해 봤다 *60, 61페이지 참조

I — have + ③

① be 있다 | ② was 있었다 | ③ been 있었었다

I have been to Spain **before**.
저는 전에 스페인에 있어 봤어요. = 저는 전에 스페인에 가 봤어요.

you — have + ③

do 하다 | did 했다 | ③ done 했었다

You have done it **once**.
당신은 그것을 한 번 해 봤어요.

we — have + ③

see 보다 | saw 봤다 | ③ seen 봤었다

We have seen the movie **twice**.
우리는 그 영화를 두 번 본 적이 있어요.

they — have + ③

hear 듣다 | heard 들었다 | ③ heard 들었었다

They have heard of it **before**.
그들은 전에 그것을 들어본 적이 있어요.

he — has + ③

eat 먹다 | ate 먹었다 | ③ eaten 먹었었다

He has eaten pizza **many times**.
그는 피자를 여러 번 먹어 봤어요.

she — has + ③

think 생각하다 | thought 생각했다 | ③ thought 생각했었다

She has never thought about it.
그녀는 그것에 대해서 생각해 본 적이 없어요.

it — has + ③

break 부서지다 | broke 부서졌다 | ③ broken 부서졌었다

It has broken in the past.
그것은 과거에 부숴졌었어요.

연습문제 — Unit 58

1. have done(~해봤다, ~한 적이 있다)을 알맞게 사용하여 문장을 완성하시오.

1) (I, see, it, before)

2) (she, be, to Spain, a couple of times)

3) (I, ride, a horse, a few times)

4) (I, try, a million times)

5) (you, meet, him, once)

6) (I, hear, of it, before)

7) (he, have a surgery, twice)

8) (my friend, stay, here, several times)

2. 주어진 단어와 have done을 사용하여 문장을 완성하시오.

(give a speech, a couple of times)   (live, for a few years)   (be, Italy, before)   (do, before)   (meet, twice)

1) I _____, but she hasn't done it yet.

2) I _____ in China _____, so I speak a little Chinese.

3) He said he _____ the President _____, but I don't trust him.

4) I _____, but I don't remember anything because I was too young.

5) I _____ in public _____, but I'm still nervous.

3. have done을 사용하여 대화을 완성하시오.

1) A: Have you ever been out of the country?   B: Yes, _____ a few times.
2) A: Have you ever sung on stage?   B: Yes, _____ since I was a kid.
3) A: Have you ever cried at school?   B: Yes, _____ at least twice.
4) A: Have you ever bought clothing online?   B: Yes, _____ many times.
5) A: Have you ever stayed up all night?   B: Yes, _____ for the last 3 days.

4. have done before를 활용하여 여러분이 해 본 경험에 대해 쓰시오.

1)   1)
2)   2)

5. have never done before를 활용하여 여러분이 한 번도 해 본 적이 없는 것을 쓰시오.

1)   1)
2)   2)

연습문제 Unit 59

1. 주어진 단어와 **have just done**을 알맞게 사용하여 문장을 완성하시오.

1) _____
(I, clean up, my room)

2) _____
(I, wake, up)

3) _____
(she, change, her, mind)

4) _____
(I, receive, an e-mail)

5) _____
(he, finish, his, homework)

6) _____
(It, begin)

7) _____
(the package, arrive)

8) _____
(we, land: 착륙하다, in Switzerland)

2. 주어진 단어와 **have already done**을 알맞게 사용하여 문장을 완성하시오.

1) _____
(he, read, the newspaper)

2) _____
(she, send, the letter)

3) _____
(he, make up his mind: 결심하다)

4) _____
(she, pass away: 돌아가시다)

5) _____
(I, have, lunch)

6) _____
(I, decide)

7) _____
(we, pay, for the tickets)

8) _____
(they, ship: 배송하다, samples)

3. 주어진 단어와 **have done**을 사용하여 대화을 완성하시오.

1) A: Did you lock the door?   B: _____ (already, lock)

2) A: You didn't know that?   B: _____ (just, notice)

3) A: Did she check out of the hotel? B: _____ (just, leave)

4) A: Is it still raining outside?   B: _____ (already, stop)

5) A: Will you send me the document? B: _____ (just, send)

4. **have just done**을 활용하여 문장을 만드시오.

1) _____

2) _____

3) _____

5. **have already done**을 활용하여 문장을 만드시오.

1) _____

2) _____

3) _____

UNIT 60

(3) I have ___
___해 왔다

*ed를 사용하지 않는 단어는 60, 61페이지 참조

I
have + ③

① visit 방문하다
② visited 방문했다
③ visited 방문했었다

I have visited 5 countries so far.
저는 지금까지 5개 국가를 방문해 왔어요.

you
have + ③

work 일하다
worked 일했다
③ worked 일했었다

You have worked here for 10 years.
당신은 여기에서 10년 동안 일해 왔어요.

we
have + ③

use 사용하다
used 사용했다
③ used 사용했었다

We have used it since the 80's.
우리는 80년대부터 그것을 사용해 왔어요.

they
have + ③

practice 연습하다
practiced 연습했다
③ practiced 연습했었다

They have practiced English for many years.
그들은 수 년동안 영어를 연습해 왔어요.

he
has + ③

work out 운동하다
worked out 운동했다
③ worked out 운동했었다

He has worked out for quite a while.
그는 꽤 오랫동안 운동해 왔어요.

she
has + ③

raise 기르다, 키우다
raised 길렀다
③ raised 길렀었다

She has raised a dog since she was 10.
그녀는 10살이었을 때부터 강아지를 길러 왔어요.

it
has + ③

take 걸리다
took 걸렸다
③ taken 걸렸었다

It has taken so many years.
그것은 수년간의 시간이 걸려 왔어요.

연습문제 — Unit 60

1. have done을 알맞게 사용하여 문장을 완성하시오. (해 왔다)

1) (I, study, English, for, a long time) _____

2) (she, travel, many countires, for, 10 years) _____

3) (we, wait, for, 30 minutes) _____

4) (they, track, your package, for, a week) _____

5) (we, have, a dog, since, 2010) _____

6) (I, know, him, since, high school) _____

7) (I, try, different ways, since, I, graduated) _____

8) (he, drive, since, he, was, 20) _____

2. 주어진 단어와 have done을 사용하여 문장을 완성하시오.

(business partners, for)   (live, I was little)   (be, since)   (graduated, run)   (for a long time, practice)

1) I know most people around here because I _____ in this town since _____.

2) We are confident enough because we _____ for the audition.

3) Peter and I _____ over 20 years. He is like family to me.

4) Elizabeth _____ a restaurant since she _____ from University.

5) The students are very tired because they _____ in the classroom _____ 8 in the morning.

3. have done을 사용하여 대화을 완성하시오.

1) 저는 지난 5년간 일기를 써 왔어요.	B: _____

2) 저는 딸이 태어났을 때부터의 동영상을 녹화해 왔어요.	B: _____

3) 그는 일을 그만둔 이후로 면접을 봐 왔어요.	B: _____

4) 그들은 여기에 도착한 이후로 회의실에 있어요.	B: _____

5) 그는 10년 동안 담배를 피워 왔어요.	B: _____

4. have done을 활용하여 여러분이 지금껏 해 온 것들을 쓰시오.

1) _____	4) _____

2) _____	5) _____

3) _____	6) _____

UNIT 61

I have been ___ing
___해 오고 있다

I — I have → I've

work 일하다
I have been working in Dubai for 2 years.
저는 두바이에서 2년동안 일해 오고 있어요.

you — you have → you've

talk 얘기하다
You have been talking for hours.
당신은 수 시간 동안 얘기해 오고 있어요.

we — we have → we've

consider 고려하다
We have been considering buying an air conditioner.
우리는 에어컨을 사는 것을 고려해 오고 있어요.

they — they have → they've

live 살다
They have been living in Hawaii since they were young.
그들은 어렸을 때부터 하와이에서 살아오고 있어요.

he — he has → he's

drive 운전하다
He has been driving since he was 18 years old.
그는 18살 때부터 운전해 오고 있어요.

she — she has → she's

wait 기다리다
She has been waiting since 2 o'clock.
그녀는 2시부터 기다려 오고 있어요.

it — it has → it's

rain 비가 내리다
It has been raining since last night.
어젯밤부터 비가 내려오고 있어요.

연습문제 　　　　　　　　　　　　　　　　　　　　Unit 61

1. have been ing를 알맞게 사용하여 문장을 완성하시오.

1) (he, stare at, me, for 5 minutes) _____

2) (I, search, for, him, since, yesterday) _____

3) (she, update, her, résumé, since, she, lose, her job) _____

4) (he, beg, me, since, he, cheat on, me) _____

5) (she, bake, for, 10 hours, straight) _____

6) (the kids, cry, since, I, get, home) _____

7) (I, think, about, you, for, a long time) _____

8) (they, working, since, last night) _____

2. 주어진 단어와 have been + ing, 또는 has been + ing를 사용하여 대화을 완성하시오.

beg	lie	change	try	look for

1) You should decide by today.　　　　I _____, but I can't decide.

2) Forgive him. He _____ you.　　　I can't. He cheated on me.

3) The world _____ quickly.　　　　Yeah. I know it's crazy.

4) Trust me. She _____ to us.　　　I thought she was a genuine person.

5) Call him. He _____ you.　　　　Why is he looking for me?

3. 주어진 단어와 have been + ing를 사용하여 문장을 완성하시오.

1) _____, and I think it's been going well.
　　(for, run, a restaurant, a month, she)

2) _____, but we still can't speak it.
　　(learn, we, years, English, for)

3) _____ since 2010.
　　(computer, I, use, this)

4) _____ since he was a student.
　　(he, here, come)

5) _____ since we broke up.
　　(I, my, avoid, ex-boyfriend)

4. have been + ing를 활용하여 학습자가 해 오고 있는 것을 쓰시오.

1) _____

2) _____

3) _____

UNIT 62

I would ___
(저라면) ___할 거예요, ___하겠어요

I ──── I would → I'd ────

I would be an architect.
(~하면) 저는 건축가가 될 거예요.

I would be grateful.
(저라면) 저는 감사할 거예요.

I would send an e-mail.
(저라면) 이메일을 보내겠어요.

you ──── you would → you'd ────

You would be an expert.
(~하면) 당신은 전문가가 될 거예요.

You would be happy.
(~하면) 당신은 행복할 거예요.

You would know.
(~하면) 당신은 알 거예요.

we ──── we would → we'd ────

We would be winners.
(~하면) 우리는 승리자가 될 거예요.

We would be sad.
(~하면) 우리는 슬플 거예요.

We would call a cop.
(~하면) 우리는 경찰을 부르겠어요.

they ──── they would → they'd ────

They would be husband and wife.
(~하면) 그들은 부부가 될 거예요.

They would be proud.
(~하면) 그들은 자랑스러워할 거예요.

They would win.
(~하면) 그들은 이기겠어요.

he ──── he would → he'd ────

He would be an analyst.
(~하면) 그는 분석가가 될 거예요.

He would be better.
(~하면) 그가 더 잘할 거예요.

He would say something.
(~하면) 그는 무언가를 말할 거예요.

she ──── she would → she'd ────

She would be an accountant.
(~하면) 그녀는 회계사가 될 거예요.

She would be late.
(~하면) 그녀는 늦을 거예요.

She would give up.
(~하면) 그녀는 포기할 거예요.

it ──── It would → It'd ────

It would be tomorrow.
(~하면) 그것은 내일일 거예요.

It would be good.
(~하면) 그것은 좋을 거예요.

It would work.
(~하면) 그것은 작동할 거예요.

연습문제 Unit 62

1. would를 알맞게 사용하여 빈 칸을 채우시오.

1) It _____ rude.
   rude: 무례하다
2) He _____ grateful.
   grateful: 고마워하다
3) It _____ great.
   great: 엄청나다
4) It _____ better.
   better: 더 좋다
5) She _____ proud of you.
   proud: 자랑스럽다
6) You _____ angry.
   angry: 화나다
7) It _____ cool.
   cool: 멋지다
8) It _____ awesome.
   awesome: 굉장하다
9) We _____ lucky.
   lucky: 운이 좋다

2. would를 알맞게 사용하여 빈 칸을 채우시오.

1) I _____ appreciate it.
   appreciate: 감사하다
2) He _____ like it.
   like: 좋아하다
3) I _____ tell her.
   tell: 말하다
4) She _____ answer.
   answer: 대답하다
5) I _____ die for you.
   die: 죽다
6) She _____ accept it.
   accept: 받아들이다
7) I _____ force him.
   force: (억지로) 하게 하다
8) He _____ ask her.
   ask: 물어 보다, 부탁하다
9) They _____ fight for it.
   fight: 싸우다

3. 괄호 안에 알맞은 말을 골라 문장을 완성하시오.

1) I think he (would, would be) work for you if you paid him $500 a month.

2) It (would be, would) nice if you could drive me home.

3) She (would, would be) appreciate it if you let her stay in your place for a night.

4) He (would be, would) answer if you (are, were) polite.

5) You (would, would be) get a chance if you (do, did) your best.

4. would와 주어진 단어를 사용하여 대화을 완성하시오.

| chase | call 911 | get revenge | unhappy | happen |

1) What would you do if someone passed out?   B: I _____
2) What if your friend betrayed you?   B: I _____
3) What if you left your phone on the bus?   B: I _____
4) What would happen if you didn't finish your homework?   B: Nothing _____
5) What would happen if you forgot your mom's birthday?   B: She _____

5. would을 사용하여 대화을 완성하시오.

1) What would you do if you lost your keys?   B: _____
2) What would you do if you won the lottery?   B: _____
3) What would you do if you were free?   B: _____
4) What would you do if you were a genius?   B: _____
5) What would you do if you were a polyglot?   B: _____

UNIT 63 Would you ___?
___해 주시겠어요?, ___하시겠어요?, ___할까요?

I ──────────────── would I ────────────────

Would I lie to her? → Why would I lie to her?
제가 그녀에게 거짓말을 하겠냐고요?

you ──────────────── would you ────────────────

Would you invite her? → Who would you invite?
(당신이라면) 그녀를 초대하시겠어요?

Would you recommend a book? → What would you recommend?
책을 추천해 주시겠어요?

we ──────────────── would we ────────────────

Would we lose the game? → Why would we lose the game?
우리가 시합에서 질까요?

they ──────────────── would they ────────────────

Would they accept it? → When would they accept it?
그들이 받아들일까요?

he ──────────────── would he ────────────────

Would he bring it? → Why would he bring it?
그가 그것을 가지고 올까요?

she ──────────────── would she ────────────────

Would she say 'yes'? → Why would she say 'no'?
그녀가 '네'라고 할까요?

it ──────────────── would it ────────────────

Would it take long? → How long would it take?
오래 걸릴까요?

연습문제 — Unit 63

1. would를 알맞게 사용하여 질문을 완성하시오. (하시겠어요?, 할까요?)

1) _____ you take the job?
   take a job: 일을 맡다
2) _____ you take him there?
   take: 데리고 가다
3) _____ he go out with her?
   go out with: ~와 사귀다
4) _____ you be upset?
   upset: 화내다
5) _____ she come back?
   come back: 돌아오다
6) _____ they pay me?
   pay: 돈을 내다
7) _____ she call me back?
   call back: 다시 전화를 하다
8) _____ it take long?
   take: (시간이) 걸리다
9) _____ you share it?
   share: 공유하다

2. 주어진 문장을 읽고 would를 사용하여 질문하시오. (하시겠어요?)

> take   call her back   grab a cab   be upset   keep

1) A: What if you missed her call? → A: Would you _____
2) A: What if you found a phone on the street? → A: Would you _____
3) A: What if you got a job offer in L.A.? → A: Would you _____
4) A: What if he doesn't show up? → B: Would you _____
5) A: What if you miss the last train? → B: Would you _____

3. would와 주어진 단어를 사용하여 대화를 완성하시오. (하시겠어요?, 할까요?)

> go   tell   know   choose   take

1) A: Please don't tell him. → B: Why ( ) I ( ) him?
2) A: I would like to go on a vacation. → B: Where ( ) you ( )?
3) A: It will take a long time. → B: How long ( ) it ( )?
4) A: We have blue, black, and white. → B: What color ( ) you ( )?
5) A: They will know. → B: How ( ) they ( )?

4. would를 알맞게 사용하여 질문을 완성하시오. (해 주시겠어요?)

1) _____ you turn it on?
   turn on: 켜다
2) _____ you turn it off?
   turn off: 끄다
3) _____ you keep it down?
   keep it down: 소리를 줄이다
4) _____ you show me around?
   show around: 구경시켜 주다
5) _____ you wait for me?
   wait: 기다리다
6) _____ clean it up?
   clean up: 청소하다

5. 주어진 문장을 읽고 would를 사용하여 질문하시오. (해 주시겠어요?)

> turn off the heater   keep it down   get rid of   consider   turn on the light

1) A: It's too dark here. → B: Would you (please) _____
2) A: It's too hot here. → B: Would you _____
3) A: It's too loud here. → B: Would you _____
4) A: We don't need this. → B: Would you _____
5) A: He wants to marry me. → B: Would you _____

UNIT 64

I would not ___
(저라면) ___안 할 거예요, ___안 하겠어요

I — would not → wouldn't

I would not be upset.
(저라면) 저는 화내지 않을 거예요.

I would not sell it.
(저라면) 그것을 팔지 않겠어요.

you — would not → wouldn't

You would not be wrong.
(~하면) 당신은 틀리지 않을 거예요.

You would not notice.
(~하면) 당신은 알아차리지 못했을 거예요.

we — would not → wouldn't

We would not be successful.
(~하면) 우리는 성공하지 않을 거예요.

We would not know.
(~하면) 우리는 알지 못했을 거예요.

they — would not → wouldn't

They would not be expensive.
(~하면) 그것들은 비싸지 않을 거예요.

They would not believe me.
(~하면) 그들은 저를 믿지 않을 거예요.

he — would not → wouldn't

(~하면) He would be better.
그가 더 나을 거예요.

He would not admit it.
(~하면) 그는 인정하지 않을 거예요.

she — would not → wouldn't

(~하면) She would be late.
그녀는 늦을 거예요.

She would not care.
(~하면) 그녀는 신경쓰지 않을 거예요.

it — would not → wouldn't

(~하면) It would not be easy.
그것은 쉽지 않을 거예요.

It would not take long.
(~하면) 그것은 오래 걸리지 않을 거예요.

연습문제 　　　　　　　　　　　　　　　　　Unit 64

1. wouldn't를 알맞게 사용하여 빈 칸을 채우시오.

1) I _____ follow him.　　2) He _____ take it seriously.　　3) I _____ lie to her.
   follow: 따라가다　　　　　　　 take: 받아들이다　　　　　　　　　 lie: 거짓말하다

4) I _____ say anything.　　5) We _____ vote for him.　　6) They _____ betray me.
   say: 말하다　　　　　　　　　　 vote: 투표하다　　　　　　　　　　 betray: 배신하다

7) I _____ tell anyone.　　9) They _____ lend me money.　　8) She _____ answer.
   tell: 말하다 (전하다)　　　　　　 lend: 빌려주다　　　　　　　　　　 answer: 대답하다

2. wouldn't을 알맞게 사용하여 문장을 완성하시오. *even if: ~라 하더라도

1) I _____ buy it even if it was $1.
2) It _____ possible without you.
3) I _____ lie to her even if I made a mistake.
4) I _____ lend him $200 if I were you.
5) You _____ here if it weren't for her.

3. 주어진 문장을 읽고 wouldn't와 주어진 단어를 사용하여 답변하시오.

> lend 　 take 　 marry 　 move 　 forgive

1) Terry is rich, but he's old. Would you marry him?　　　　No, _____
2) You are going to be late for work. Would you take a taxi?　　No, _____
3) You should move to Busan to get your dream job. Would you?　No, _____
4) Your best friend asked for $1,000. Would you lend it to him?　No, _____
5) Your girlfriend cheated on you. Would you break up with her?　Yes, _____

4. 주어진 문장을 읽고 wouldn't을 사용하여 답변하시오.

1) Would you get a puppy?　　　　　　　　　No, _____
2) Would you give up everything for love?　　　No, _____
3) Would you lend your friend a car?　　　　　 No, _____
4) Would you pay $1,000 for shoes?　　　　　　No, _____
5) Would you drink coffee instead of water?　　No, _____

UNIT 65

If ___
만약 ___면/으면

I / if I

were

I wouldn't do it **if I** were you.
제가 당신이라면 그것을 안 할 거예요.

do/did

I am sorry **if I** made a mistake.
제가 실수했다면 죄송해요.

you / if you

I would be happy **if you** were here.
당신이 여기에 있으면 저는 행복할 거예요.

It will be great **if you** go there.
당신이 그곳에 간다면 굉장할 거예요.

we / if we

It would be good **if we** were close.
우리가 친하면 좋을 거예요.

It will be amazing **if we** win the lottery.
우리가 복권에 당첨된다면 놀라울 거예요.

they / if they

It would be awesome **if they** were mine.
그것들이 나의 것이면 정말 좋을 거예요.

I won't forgive them **if they** use me.
그들이 저를 이용한다면 저는 그들을 용서하지 않을 거예요.

he / if he

We would be in trouble **if he** weren't here.
그가 여기에 없으면 우리는 곤란할 거예요.

He would help you **if he** could.
그가 할 수 있었다면 당신을 도왔을 거예요.

she / if she

She would be in trouble **if she** were late.
그녀가 늦으면 (그녀는) 곤란할 거예요.

I won't be angry **if she** helps me.
그녀가 저를 도운다면 저는 화내지 않을 거예요.

it / if it

I would buy it **if it** were cheap.
그것이 (값이) 싸면 살 거예요.

It would be cool **if** animals could speak.
동물들이 말할 수 있었다면 멋졌을 거예요.

연습문제 Unit 65

1. if와 주어진 단어를 사용하여 문장을 완성하시오.

1) I would go to the party _____ (I, you)
2) I would save the world _____ (I, a superhero)
3) I would buy a nice car _____ (I, millionaire)
4) It would be better _____ (if, free)
5) It would be easy _____ (she, here)

2. if와 주어진 단어를 사용하여 문장을 완성하시오.

1) I would travel more _____ (I, young)
2) You wouldn't do it _____ (it, hard)
3) We would get it _____ (we, lucky)
4) They would forget the word _____ (it, too long)
5) I wouldn't be mad _____ (they, nice)

3. if와 주어진 단어를 알맞게 사용하여 문장을 완성하시오.

1) I will call you _____ (I, find out, found out)
2) They will consider it _____ (showed, you, them, show)
3) She will regret it _____ (she, it, didn't, doesn't, do)
4) It will work _____ (he, fixed, it, fixes)
5) He will be very disappointed _____ (don't, show up, you, didn't)

4. 주어진 단어와 if를 사용하여 대화를 완성하시오.

> (get)   (go)   (do)   (help)   (get)

1) Should I buy this for her?   You should ( ) it ( ) she likes it.
2) Are you going there?   I'm ( )ing ( ) you are going.
3) Can you do it for me?   I will ( ) it ( ) you want me to.
4) Will you get it for her?   I will go ( ) it ( ) she needs it.
5) Do I have to help them?   You have to ( ) them ( ) you can.

3. would와 if를 사용하여 질문에 답하시오.

1) What would you do if you had a time machine? _____
2) What would you do if things weren't going well? _____
3) What would you buy if you were rich? _____
4) Where would you go if you were free? _____
5) Would you be happy if you were single? _____

UNIT 66

When I ___
저는 ___ㄹ 때/을 때

I

I am not happy when I am hungry.
저는 배고플 때 행복하지 않아요.

I am not happy when I study.
저는 공부할 때 행복하지 않아요.

I went to college when I was 20.
저는 20살이었을 때 대학교에 갔어요.

It was 2'o clock when I got here.
제가 여기에 도착했을 때 2시였어요.

you

You were fast when you were young.
당신은 젊었을 때 빨랐어요.

I was taking a shower when you called.
당신이 전화했을 때 저는 샤워를 하고 있었어요.

we

He was our hero when we were little.
우리가 작았을 때 그는 우리의 영웅이었어요.

It was 2017 when we met.
우리가 만났을 때 2017년이었어요.

they

I was not here when they were here.
그들이 여기에 있었을 때. 저는 여기에 없었어요.

She was crying when they came.
그들이 왔을 때 그녀는 울고 있었어요.

he

She was there when he was sick.
그가 아팠을 때 그녀는 그곳에 있었어요.

She was waiting when he was working.
그가 일할 때 그녀는 기다리고 있었어요.

she

She felt sorry when she was late.
그녀가 늦었을 때 그녀는 미안함을 느꼈어요.

I was singing when she was driving.
그녀가 운전하고 있었을 때 저는 노래를 하고 있었어요.

it

Nobody was there when it was dark.
어두웠을 때 그곳에 아무도 없었어요.

I was inside when it was raining.
비가 내리고 있었을 때 저는 안에 있었어요.

연습문제 — Unit 66

1. when과 주어진 단어를 사용하여 문장을 완성하시오.

1) I am happy _____ (you, smile)
   smile: 미소 짓다
2) I can't focus _____ (he, here)
   here: 여기
3) Call me _____ (you, have time)
   have time: 시간이 있다
4) I will do it _____ (I, free)
   free: 자유롭다
5) Take a pill _____ (you, sick)
   take a pill: 약을 먹다
6) She is quiet _____ (she, work)
   quiet: 조용하다

2. when과 주어진 단어를 사용하여 문장을 완성하시오.

1) I was stupid _____ (I, young)
   young: 젊다
2) He was leaving _____ (I, see, him)
   see: 보다
3) She was short _____ (she, student)
   short: 키가 작다
4) We were poor _____ (you, little)
   little: 작다
5) I wanted to be a pilot _____ (I, 15)
   15: 15살
6) I didn't know _____ (I, kid)
   kid: 아이

3. when과 주어진 단어를 알맞게 사용하여 문장을 완성하시오.

1) Let me know _____ (hang out, you, want to)

2) I will let you know _____ (am, available, I, was)

3) She was resting _____ (is, was, working, he)

4) It was 9 in the morning _____ (I, woke up, wake up)

5) What should I do _____ (slept, can't, I, sleep,)

4. when을 사용하여 질문에 답하시오.

1) What do you do when you are bored?
2) What were you doing when it was 6 in the morning?
3) What do you usually do when you have time?
4) When do you practice English?
5) When do you take a taxi?

5. when을 사용하여 나의 과거에 대하여 작문하시오.

UNIT 67

There is ___
___이 있어요

a ········· there is → there's ·········

There is a guy → There is a guy in my room.
(거기에) 한 남자가 있어요   제 방에 한 남자가 있어요.

There is a book → There is a book on the desk.
(거기에) 책이 있어요   책상 위에 책이 있어요.

Un-countable ········· there is → there's ·········

There is water → There is so much water.   There is a lot of water.
물이 있어요   아주 많은 물이 있어요.   많은 물이 있어요.

There is something.   There is someone.   There is no one.
무언가가 있어요.   누군가가 있어요.   아무도 없어요.
↕   =   =
There is nothing.   There is somebody.   There is nobody.
아무것도 없어요.   누군가가 있어요.   아무도 없어요.

There are ___
___들이 있어요

s ········· there are ·········

There are cars → There are many cars. → There are many cars on the road.
자동차들이 있어요   많은 자동차들이 있어요.   도로에 많은 자동차들이 있어요.

countable ········· there are ·········

There are lots of things.   There are a lot of flowers.   There are dozens of participants.
많은 것들이 있어요.   꽃들이 많이 있어요.   수십 명의 참가자들이 있어요.

There are loads of boxes.   There are hundreds of people.   There are plenty of tomatoes.
많은 상자들이 있어요.   수 백명의 사람들이 있어요.   토마토들이 많이 있어요.

연습문제 — Unit 67

1. there is, there are를 사용하여 문장을 완성하시오.

1) _____ a book on the desk.
2) _____ something on your face.
3) _____ a lot of people at the club.
4) _____ no money in my bank account.
5) _____ a famous restaurant in this town.
6) _____ two cats under the chair.
7) _____ a fan next to the couch.
8) _____ many dogs in front of the door.
9) _____ so much sand in the desert.
10) _____ a reason why I didn't tell her.

2. there is, there are를 사용하여 문장을 완성하시오.

1) _____ nothing to do.
2) _____ so much to learn.
3) _____ a lot to do.
4) _____ many things to enjoy.

3. there is, there are를 사용하여 문장을 완성하시오.

1) _____ something I didn't tell you.
2) _____ always something we can do.
3) _____ someone you need to meet.
4) _____ something I want to buy.
5) _____ no one on the street.
6) _____ nothing we can do.
7) _____ something we should talk about.
8) _____ somebody I would like to introduce.
9) _____ something I have to tell you.
10) _____ nobody here.

4. there is, there are를 사용하여 문장을 완성하시오.

1) _____ so much hair on the floor.
2) _____ lots of users.
3) _____ plenty of possiblities.
4) _____ loads of dishes in the sink.
5) _____ many ways.
6) _____ a lot of reasons.
7) _____ only one thing you should know.
8) _____ hundreds of opportunities.

UNIT 68 that, who, which
는

는 ──────────── **that** *사람, 사물 둘 다 사용 ────────────

This is a computer.　+　I use it.
이것은 컴퓨터예요.　　저는 그것을 사용해요.

This is the computer that I use ~~it~~.
이것은 제가 ~~그것을~~ 사용하는 컴퓨터예요.

ㄴ, 은 ──────────── **that** ────────────

This is a computer.　+　I used it.
이것은 컴퓨터예요.　　저는 그것을 사용했어요.

This is the computer that I used ~~it~~.
이것은 제가 ~~그것을~~ 사용한 컴퓨터예요.

ㄹ, 을 ──────────── **that** ────────────

This is a computer.　+　I am going to use it.
이것은 컴퓨터예요.　　저는 그것을 사용할 거예요.

This is the computer that I am going to use ~~it~~.
이것은 제가 ~~그것을~~ 사용할 컴퓨터예요.

는 ──────────── **who** *사람에게만 사용 ────────────

This is a student.　+　He lives in China.
이 사람은 학생이에요.　　그는 중국에서 살아요.

This is a student who ~~he~~ lives in China.
이 사람은 ~~그는~~ 중국에서 사는 학생이에요.

는 ──────────── **which** *사물에만 사용 ────────────

This is a computer.　+　I use it.
이것은 컴퓨터예요.　　저는 그것을 사용해요.

This is the computer which I use ~~it~~.
이것은 제가 ~~그것을~~ 사용하는 컴퓨터예요.

연습문제 Unit 68

1. that을 활용하여 두 문장을 한 문장으로 연결하시오.

1) This is the car. I like it.

2) These are the cups. We share them.

3) Here is the map. It shows the island.

4) This is the movie. My dad likes it.

5) My mom has a new skirt. She wears it every day.

2. that을 활용하여 두 문장을 한 문장으로 연결하시오.

1) That is the book. You have to read it.

2) That is the problem. I can't figure it out.

3) Here is the picture. I want you to see it.

4) There is something important. I have to tell you.

5) This is the jacket. I bought it in France.

3. who를 활용하여 두 문장을 한 문장으로 연결하시오.

1) There is a guy. I met him in Australia.

2) I am a student. I am looking for a job.

3) She is the one. She gave me a chance.

4) He is the guy. He wrote a book.

5) I have to find someone. She can help me.

4. who, that, which를 알맞게 활용하여 두 문장을 한 문장으로 연결하시오.

1) She is the woman. I love her.

2) She is the girl. I want to marry her.

3) I have friends. They live in Switzerland.

4) I have evidence. It can prove it.

5) I have a cat. I got it at a shelter.

UNIT 69 자주 쓰는 문법

It's easy to ___
___기 쉽다

It is easy to say.
말하기는 쉽죠.

It is easy to forget.
잊어버리기 쉬워요.

It is easy to use.
사용하기 쉬워요.

It's difficult to ___
___기 어렵다

It is difficult to understand.
이해하기 어려워요.

It is difficult to describe.
묘사하기 어려워요.

It is difficult to fix.
고치기 어려워요.

It's hard to ___
___기 힘들다

It is hard to get.
얻기 힘들어요.

It is hard to explain.
설명하기 힘들어요.

It is hard to guess.
추측하기 힘들어요.

I start ___ing
___기 시작하다

I started building a house.
저는 집을 짓기 시작했어요.

They started fighting.
그들은 싸우기 시작했어요.

She started crying.
그녀는 울기 시작했어요.

I stop ___ing
___기를 멈추다/그만하다

I stopped smoking.
저는 담배를 끊었어요.

She stopped talking.
그녀는 얘기하는 것을 멈췄어요.

We stopped seeing each other.
우리는 헤어졌어요.

keep ___ing
계속해서 ___하다

I kept walking.
저는 계속해서 걸었어요.

They kept arguing.
그들은 계속해서 말다툼을 했어요.

He kept shouting.
그는 계속해서 소리쳤어요.

I am good at ___
___을 잘하다

I'm good at math.
저는 수학을 잘해요.

She is good at driving.
그녀는 운전을 잘해요.

We are good at dancing.
우리는 춤을 잘 춰요.

I like ___ing
___기를 좋아하다

I like cooking.
저는 요리하기를 좋아해요.
→ 저는 요리를 좋아해요.

She likes drawing.
그녀는 그리기를 좋아해요.

He likes swimming.
그는 수영하기를 좋아해요.
→ 저는 수영을 좋아해요.

I like to ___
___하는 것을 좋아하다

I like to cook.
저는 요리하는 것을 좋아해요.

She likes to draw.
그녀는 그리는 것을 좋아해요.

He likes to swim.
그는 수영하는 것을 좋아해요.

I would like to ___
___고 싶습니다

I would like to cancel.
저는 취소하고 싶습니다.

We would like to apologize.
우리는 사과하고 싶습니다.

She would like to join us.
그녀는 우리와 함께하고 싶어합니다.

like ___
___처럼, ___같이

I work like a slave.
저는 노예처럼 일해요.

She eats like a bird.
그녀는 새처럼 먹어요.

I feel like I'm dreaming.
꿈을 꾸고 있는 것 같이 느껴져요.

I am like ___
___같아요

I am like a soldier.
저는 군인같아요.

She is like family.
그녀는 가족같아요.

He is like a baby.
그는 아기같아요.

I like ___
___을 좋아하다

I like animals.
저는 동물을 좋아해요.

She likes cats.
그녀는 고양이를 좋아해요.

He likes dogs.
그는 개를 좋아해요.

like this
이렇게, 이런 식으로

Do it like this.
이렇게 하세요.

Do it like that.
저렇게 하세요.

Don't treat me like that.
저를 그런 식으로 대하지 마세요.

UNIT 70 자주 쓰는 표현

It's up to you.
당신에게 달렸어요.

It's your call.
당신에게 달렸어요.

Be my guest.
좋을 대로 하세요.

Who's up for darts?
다트할 사람?

I'm down.
기꺼이 할래요.

I'm in.
저는 할래요.

Let's grab some beer.
맥주 한 잔 합시다.

I got wasted last night.
어젯밤에 만취했어요.

I'm out.
저는 빠질게요.

I got hammered last night.
어젯밤에 만취했어요.

Let's split the bill.
비용을 각자 부담합시다.

It's on me.
제가 낼게요

Don't get me wrong.
오해하지 마세요.

Wish me luck.
저에게 행운을 빌어 주세요.

So far so good.
지금까지는 좋아요.

Let's get to know each other.
서로를 알아갑시다.

My phone is running out of battery.
제 핸드폰의 배터리가 떨어지고 있어요.

I will hit you up later.
내가 나중에 연락할게.

Let's keep in touch.
서로 연락하고 지내자.

What have I done?
내가 무슨 짓을 한 거지?

What's that?
뭐라고?

How come?
어쩌다가?

I'm getting there.
거의 다 되어 가고 있어요.

I'm on my way.
가는 중이에요.

I'm working on it.
작업 중이에요.

Make it happen!
꼭 이루어 내세요!

Ta-da
짜잔

Shush!
쉿! 조용!

Ouch!
아이고!

Ew!
우웩!

Oops!
어맛!

Boom!
쾅!

That's it. 그게 다예요.	**That's all.** 그게 다예요.	**Fair enough.** 그래요. 좋아요.
Have a look. 한 번 보세요.	**Take a look.** 한 번 보세요.	**Check it out.** 확인해 보세요.
What's going on? 무슨 일이에요?	**As far as I know ...** 제가 알기로는 ...	**Stop it.** 그만 좀 하세요.
We are meant to be together. 우리는 함께할 운명이에요.	**I mean..** 그러니까 내 말은..	**I mean it.** 정말이에요.
Sounds good. 그래요. 좋아요.	**That's awesome!** 대박이네요!	**Brilliant!** 엄청나네요!
You killed it. 완전 끝내줬어요.	**You nailed it.** 성공적이었어요.	**You made it.** 당신이 해냈어요.
Well done. 잘했어요.	**Good job.** 잘했어요.	**There you go.** 잘했어요./여기요.
For real? 진짜로?	**For sure?** 확실해요?	**Are you sure?** 확실해요?
No way. 말도 안 돼!	**That's ridiculous!** 말도 안 돼!	**Indeed.** 정말로, 실제로
Hold on. 잠깐만요.	**Hang on.** 기다려요.	**Wait on.** 기다리세요.
One moment. 잠깐만요.	**One second.** 잠시만요.	**One minute.** 1분만 주세요.
Hop in! 타세요!	**Pull over.** (차를) 대세요.	**Slow down.** 속도를 줄이세요.
What's wrong with you? 도대체 왜 그러시는 거예요?	**For good.** 영원히.	**What for?** 뭐때문에요?, 뭐 하려고요?

Final Test 1

1. How are you (   )? **Unit 4**
A. going   B. doing   C. do   D. long time

2. What have you been (   )? **Unit 4**
A. while   B. going   C. up to   D. down to

3. 75,000 **Unit 5**
A. seventy five thousand   B. seven five thousand   C. seventy thousand five thousand

4. 8월 **Unit 6**
A. October   B. September   C. November   D. August

5. 수요일 **Unit 6**
A. Tuesday   B. Wednesday   C. Saturday   D. Monday

6. She (   ) a professor. **Unit 7**
A. does   B. am   C. are   D. is

7. They (   ) adorable. **Unit 7**
A. are   B. is   C. am   D. be

8. Where (   ) you? **Unit 8**
A. do   B. does   C. is   D. are

9. (   ) he cool? **Unit 8**
A. does   B. do   C. is   D. it

10. I (   ) (   ) a teenager. **Unit 9**
A. am, not   B. am, a   C. do, not   D. does, not

11. We (   ) (   ) comfortable. **Unit 9**
A. are, a   B. are, not   C. do, not   D. is, not

158

12. We (　　　) everyday.　　　　　　　　　　　　　　　　　Unit 10
　A. work　　B. works　　C. are work　　D. does work

13. He (　　) in Mexico.　　　　　　　　　　　　　　　　　　Unit 10
　A. do live　　B. live　　C. lives　　D. is live

14. What (　　　) you do?　　　　　　　　　　　　　　　　　Unit 11
　A. are　　B. do　　C. does　　D. is

15. (　　　) she drink?　　　　　　　　　　　　　　　　　　Unit 11
　A. do　　B. does　　C. is　　D. are

16. I (　　　) think so.　　　　　　　　　　　　　　　　　　Unit 12
　A. am not　　B. does　　C. doesn't　　D. don't

17. She goes (　　　) church.　　　　　　　　　　　　　　　Unit 13
　A. in　　B. on　　C. to　　D. at

18. I go to the cafe (　　　) drink coffee with my friend .　　Unit 13
　A. to　　B. for　　C. on　　D. in

19. People share ideas (　　　) solve a problem.　　　　　　Unit 13
　A. for　　B. to　　C. by　　D. from

20. I swear (　　　) God.　　　　　　　　　　　　　　　　　Unit 13
　A. on　　B. for　　C. to　　D. from

21. I go to work from Mondays (　　　) Fridays.　　　　　　Unit 13
　A. from　　B. on　　C. to　　D. at

22. They come to Korea (　　　) March.　　　　　　　　　　Unit 14
　A. in　　B. on　　C. at　　D. by

159

23. I buy things (　　) the Internet.　　　　　　　　　　　　Unit 14
　　A. in　　B. on　　C. at　　D. from

24. She is (　　) the gym.　　　　　　　　　　　　　　　　　Unit 14
　　A. on　　B. at　　C. in　　D. to

25. They are (　　) children.　　　　　　　　　　　　　　　Unit 15
　　A. him　　B. them　　C. mine　　D. my

26. Do you remember (　　)?　　　　　　　　　　　　　　Unit 15
　　A. he　　B. his　　C. she　　D. her

27. (　　) nice.　　　　　　　　　　　　　　　　　　　　　Unit 16
　　A. Be　　B. Am　　C. Are　　D. Is

28. Don't (　　).　　　　　　　　　　　　　　　　　　　　Unit 16
　　A. be hesitate　　B. hesitate　　C. hesitated　　D. be hesitated

29. She never (　　).　　　　　　　　　　　　　　　　　　Unit 17
　　A. laugh　　B. laughs　　C. be laugh　　D. be laughs

30. They usually (　　) here around 10.　　　　　　　　　Unit 17
　　A. come　　B. comes　　C. be come　　D. be comes

31. Let's (　　).　　　　　　　　　　　　　　　　　　　　Unit 18
　　A. sees　　B. seen　　C. saw　　D. see

32. Let's not (　　) it.　　　　　　　　　　　　　　　　　Unit 18
　　A. do　　B. did　　C. done　　D. does

33. Let (　　) guess.　　　　　　　　　　　　　　　　　　Unit 18
　　A. I　　B. my　　C. me　　D. mine

34. You (   ) amazing. Unit 19
 A. was   B. were   C. be   D. is

35. She (   ) a teacher. Unit 19
 A. was   B. were   C. are   D. be

36. (   ) it difficult? Unit 20
 A. was   B. were   C. be   D. are

37. They (   ) wrong. Unit 19
 A. was   B. were   C. 's   D. is

38. She (   ) my hero. Unit 19
 A. be   B. am   C. was   D. were

39. Where (   ) it? Unit 20
 A. am   B. are   C. was   D. were

40. How much (   ) it? Unit 20
 A. this   B. was   C. that   D. it

41. He (   ) polite. Unit 21
 A. were   B. weren't   C. wasn't   D. be not

42. It (   ) my idea. Unit 21
 A. wasn't   B. were   C. weren't   D. be not

43. I (   ) basketball yesterday. Unit 22
 A. play   B. played   C. plaid   D. playd

44. I (   ) it last week. Unit 23
 A. do   B. did   C. done   D. didn't

161

45. How did you guys (   )?   Unit 24
　A. meet　　B. met　　C. meeted　　D. meted

46. I (   ) say anything.   Unit 25
　A. did　　B. didn't　　C. am not　　D. was not

47. I came back (   ) you.   Unit 26
　A. in　　B. on　　C. at　　D. for

48. These tools are (   ) making furniture.   Unit 26
　A. for　　B. to　　C. on　　D. of

49. We tried (   ) a week.   Unit 26
　A. on　　B. of　　C. for　　D. at

50. She (   ) out loud.   Unit 27
　A. laugh　　B. is laugh　　C. was laugh　　D. is laughing

51. Something (   ).   Unit 27
　A. are happen　　B. are happening　　C. was happen　　D. is happening

52. Are you (   ) fun?   Unit 28
　A. have　　B. has　　C. having　　D. be

53. He's not (   ).   Unit 29
　A. kid　　B. kidding　　C. kiding　　D. be kidding

54. I was just (   ) around.   Unit 30
　A. looking　　B. look　　C. looked　　D. be looking

55. (   ) you (   ) to me?   Unit 31
　A. are, listen　　B. were, listen　　C. were, listened　　D. were, listening

56. They (　　) not (　　) attention.　　　　　　　　　　　　　　　　**Unit 32**
　A. are, pay　　B. don't, pay　　C. do, paying　　D. are, paying

57. We (　　) (　　) make it.　　　　　　　　　　　　　　　　　　　**Unit 33**
　A. going, to　　B. are, going to　　C. are, go to　　D. go, to

58. He (　　) (　　) deal with it.　　　　　　　　　　　　　　　　　**Unit 33**
　A. is, going to　　B. is, go　　C. does, going　　D. doesn't, going to

59. (　　) you (　　) take his class?　　　　　　　　　　　　　　　**Unit 34**
　A. Do, go to　　B. Do, going to　　C. Are, going to　　D. Are, go to

60. How long (　　) she (　　) stay here?　　　　　　　　　　　　**Unit 34**
　A. does, go to　　B. is, go to　　C. does, going to　　D. is, going to

61. It (　　) not (　　) difficult.　　　　　　　　　　　　　　　　　**Unit 35**
　A. is, going to　　B. is, going to be　　C. does, going to be　　D. does, going to

62. I will (　　) that in mind.　　　　　　　　　　　　　　　　　　　**Unit 36**
　A. keep　　B. keeping　　C. kept　　D. going to, keep

63. Will you (　　) this for me?　　　　　　　　　　　　　　　　　　**Unit 37**
　A. watch　　B. watching　　C. watched　　D. going to, watch

64. Trust me. I won't (　　) you down.　　　　　　　　　　　　　　**Unit 38**
　A. let　　B. letting　　C. let's　　D. going to, let

65. You can (　　) anything.　　　　　　　　　　　　　　　　　　　**Unit 39**
　A. doing　　B. did　　C. does　　D. do

66. Can I (　　) you something?　　　　　　　　　　　　　　　　　**Unit 40**
　A. asking　　B. asks　　C. ask　　D. asked

67. I can't (   ) it. Unit 41
　A. afford　　B. affording　　C. afforded　　D. be afford

68. She (   ) a model. Unit 42
　A. want to　　B. wants to　　C. want to be　　D. wants to be

69. We (   ) travel all around the world. Unit 42
　A. want　　B. want to　　C. wants to　　D. want to be

70. What does he (   ) do for his birthday? Unit 43
　A. want　　B. wants　　C. want to　　D. wants to

71. I don't (   ) a liar. Unit 44
　A. want to　　B. wants to　　C. want to be　　D. wants to be

72. I (   ) you to check this out. Unit 45
　A. want　　B. want to　　C. want to be　　D. wants

73. Do you want (   ) to leave? Unit 46
　A. I　　B. my　　C. me　　D. mine

74. She doesn't want (   ) to stay here. Unit 47
　A. we　　B. our　　C. ours　　D. us

75. They (   ) get up early tomorrow. Unit 48
　A. need　　B. need to　　C. needs to　　D. are need to

76. Do we (   ) go to university? Unit 49
　A. need to　　B. needs to　　C. need　　D. needs

77. You don't (   ) study for exams. Unit 50
　A. need　　B. needs　　C. need to　　D. needs to

78. You (   ) confident.   Unit 51
   A. have to   B. has to   C. has to be   D. have to be

79. How many times do I (   ) explain it?   Unit 52
   A. have to   B. have to be   C. has to   D. has to be

80. You (   ) (   ) worry about it.   Unit 53
   A. don't, has to   B. don't, have to   C. doesn't has to   D. doesn't, have to

81. We (   ) quiet in public places.   Unit 54
   A. shouldn't   B. shouldn't be   C. should   D. should be

82. Where (   ) we meet?   Unit 55
   A. should   B. shouldn't   C. should be   D. shouldn't be

83. You (   ) here.   Unit 56
   A. should   B. shouldn't   C. shouldn't be   D. are should be

84. We (   ) remember.   Unit 57
   A. must be   B. must   C. musts   D. are must

85. I (   ) just changed my mind.   Unit 58
   A. have   B. has   C. am have   D. had

86. We have (   ) many times.   Unit 59
   A. try   B. trying   C. tried   D. tryed

87. I have (   ) of it.   Unit 60
   A. hear   B. heard   C. heared   D. hearing

88. It has been (   ) me.   Unit 61
   A. follow   B. following   C. followed   D. follows

89. It (   ) great. Unit 62
  A. would   B. would be   C. woudn't   D. would have

90. (   ) turn on the light for me? Unit 63
  A. would I   B. would you   C. would we   D. would

91. How long (   ) it take? Unit 63
  A. wouldn't   B. woudn't be   C. would   D. would be

92. I (   ) lie to her if I were you. Unit 64
  A. would be   B. wouldn't be   C. wouldn't   D. would have

93. Will you take me to a fancy restaurant (   ) you? Unit 65
  A. if I visit   B. if I visited   C. if I am visiting   D. if I was visiting

94. I will give you a call (   ) her. Unit 66
  A. when I see   B. when I saw   C. when I have seen   D. when I was seeing

95. (   ) a problem. Unit 67
  A. There   B. There's   C. There are   D. There were

96. (   ) something to eat? Unit 67
  A. There is   B. Is there   C. There are   D. Are there

97. There (   ) many people. Unit 67
  A. is   B. are   C. was   D. too

98. (   ) there a lot of people? Unit 67
  A. Are   B. Is   C. Were   D. Be

99. This is a letter (   ) I got from my girlfriend. Unit 68
  A. who   B. that   C. they   D. whom

100. Do you (　　) me to (　　)?
A. want, pull over   B. wants, pulls over   C. want to, pull over   D. wanted, pull over

101. Can I (　　) your car?
A. borrow   B. borrows   C. borrowed   D. be borrow

102. I (　　) (　　) to the Philippines once.
A. have, be   B. have, been   C. has, be   D. has, been

103. I am here (　　) pick up my luggage.
A. in   B. on   C. for   D. to

104. Please (　　) up the form.
A. feel   B. fill   C. pill   D. full

105. I am (　　) you.
A. warn   B. warned   C. warning   D. be warn

106. You (　　) curse here.
A. shoulnd't be   B. shouldn't   C. should be   D. should have

107. At what time (　　) you get here?
A. is   B. are   C. have   D. did

108. How long (　　) you been here?
A. do   B. are   C. have   D. did

109. (　　) you speak English?
A. Are   B. Do   C. Is   D. Be

110. We can (　　) anything.
A. do   B. did   C. does   D. done

Final Test 2

1. 'am, are, is'를 사용하여 문장을 만드시오.

2. 'am, are, is'를 사용하여 질문을 만드시오.

3. 'am, are, is'와 'not'을 사용하여 문장을 만드시오.

4. 'do, does'를 사용하여 문장을 만드시오.

5. 'do'와 'I, you, we, they, he, she, it'을 사용하여 질문을 만드시오.

6. 'I, you, we, they, he, she, it'와 'do, does', 'not'을 사용하여 문장을 만드시오.

7. 'to'를 사용하여 문장을 만드시오.

8. 'in'을 사용하여 문장을 만드시오.

9. 'on'을 사용하여 문장을 만드시오.

10. 'at'을 사용하여 문장을 만드시오.

11. 'my'를 사용하여 문장을 만드시오.

12. 'me'를 사용하여 문장을 만드시오.

13. 'mine'를 사용하여 문장을 만드시오.

14. 'your'을 사용하여 문장을 만드시오.

15. 'yours'를 사용하여 문장을 만드시오.

16. 'his'을 사용하여 문장을 만드시오.

17. 'him'을 사용하여 문장을 만드시오.

18. 'her'를 사용하여 문장을 만드시오.

19. 'our'을 사용하여 문장을 만드시오.

20. 'us'을 사용하여 문장을 만드시오.

21. 'their'을 사용하여 문장을 만드시오.

22. 'them'를 사용하여 문장을 만드시오.

Final Test 2 - 2

23. 'do'를 사용하여 명령하는 문장을 만드시오.

24. 'don't do'를 사용하여 명령하는 문장을 만드시오.

25. 'always'를 사용하여 문장을 만드시오.

26. 'sometimes'를 사용하여 문장을 만드시오.

27. 'often'을 사용하여 문장을 만드시오.

28. 'Let's'를 사용하여 문장을 만드시오.

29. 'Let's not'을 사용하여 문장을 만드시오.

30. ' was, were'를 사용하여 문장을 만드시오.

31. 'was, were'을 사용하여 질문을 만드시오.

32. 'was, were', 'not'을 사용하여 문장을 만드시오.

33. 'ed'를 사용하여 문장을 만드시오.

34. 'did'를 사용하여 질문을 만드시오.

35. 'be going to'를 사용하여 문장을 만드시오.

36. 'be going to'을 사용하여 질문을 만드시오.

37. 'am/are/is not going to'를 사용하여 문장을 만드시오.

38. 'will'을 사용하여 문장을 만드시오.

39. 'will'을 사용하여 질문을 만드시오.

40. 'will not'을 사용하여 문장을 만드시오.

41. 'can'을 사용하여 문장을 만드시오.

42. 'can'을 사용하여 질문을 만드시오.

43. 'can not'을 사용하여 문장을 만드시오.

44. 'want to'를 사용하여 문장을 만드시오.

Final Test 2 - 3

45. 'do/does', 'want to'를 사용하여 질문을 만드시오.

46. 'don't want to, doesn't want to'를 사용하여 문장을 만드시오.

47. 'want someone to'를 사용하여 문장을 만드시오.

48. 'want someone to'를 사용하여 질문을 만드시오.

49. 'don't/doesn't want someone to'를 사용하여 문장을 만드시오.

50. 'need to'를 사용하여 문장을 만드시오.

51. 'don't/doesn't need to'을 사용하여 문장을 만드시오.

52. 'need to'를 사용하여 질문을 만드시오.

53. 'don't/doesn't need to'를 사용하여 질문을 만드시오.

54. 'have to'를 사용하여 문장을 만드시오.

55. 'have to'를 사용하여 질문을 만드시오.

56. 'don't/doesn't have to'를 사용하여 문장을 만드시오.

57. 'should'를 사용하여 문장을 만드시오.

58. 'should'를 사용하여 질문을 만드시오.

59. 'should not'을 사용하여 문장을 만드시오.

60. 'must'을 사용하여 문장을 만드시오.

61. 'have done(해 봤다)'을 사용하여 문장을 만드시오.

62. 'have done(다 했다)'을 사용하여 문장을 만드시오.

63. 'have done(해 왔다)'을 사용하여 문장을 만드시오.

64. 'have been ing'를 사용하여 문장을 만드시오.

65. 'would'를 사용하여 문장을 만드시오.

66. 'would'를 사용하여 질문을 만드시오.

Final Test 2 - 4

67. 'would not'을 사용하여 문장을 만드시오.

68. 'don't want to, doesn't want to'를 사용하여 문장을 만드시오.

69. 'if'를 사용하여 문장을 만드시오.

70. 'when'을 사용하여 질문을 만드시오.

71. 'there is'를 사용하여 문장을 만드시오.

72. 'there are'를 사용하여 문장을 만드시오.

73. 'that'을 사용하여 두 문장을 한 문장으로 만드시오.

74. 'who'을 사용하여 두 문장을 한 문장으로 만드시오.

75. 'which'을 사용하여 두 문장을 한 문장으로 만드시오.

정답

UNIT 04

1.
1) Long time no see./It's been a while./It's been a long time.
2) I apologize.
3) Good job, Well done.
4) See you soon.
5) How have you been?
6) Congratulations.
7) How's it going?
8) Have a nice day.
9) No worries./No problem./It's alright.
10) Excuse me.
11) Take it easy.
12) Excuse me?, I am sorry?
13) What are you up to?
14) Not much.
15) Be careful.

2.
1) 5)
2) 1)
3) 4)
4) 2)
5) 3)

3.
1) 1)
2) 4)
3) 5)
4) 2)
5) 3)

UNIT 05

1.
1) two
2) four
3) three
4) twelve
5) twenty
6) seventy-six
7) two hundred two
8) four hundred seventy
9) nine hundred twenty-seven
10) two thousand, six hundred
11) seven thousand, three hundred fifty
12) four thousand, three hundred seventy-one
13) fifty thousand
14) seventy-eight thousand
15) ninety-three thousand four hundred

2. 예)
1) two thousand twenty
2) thirty-four
3) zero one zero two seven four eight six two zero five
4) ten thousand Won
5) twelve fourteen

3. 예)
1) zero one zero five seven two eight three four one six
2) zero one zero one four four nine seven one eight two
3) zero one zero three five four nine four two zero three

4. 예)
1) 23rd floor
2) 8th floor
3) 33rd birthday
4) the 21st century
5) 4th week

UNIT 06

1.
1) It's 5 o'clock.
2) It's three fifty five.
3) It's one forty.
4) It's nine O five.
5) It's ten thirty.

2.
1) It's Wednesday
2) It's July thirteenth
3) It's Febraury
4) It's two thousand twenty five

3.
1) one O five
2) two twenty
3) three forty five
4) four seventeen
5) five thirty
6) six oh nine
7) seven forty one
8) eight fifty
9) nine twelve
10) ten ten
11) eleven o'clock
12) twelve O three
13) eight fourteen
14) seven twenty-eight
15) one eighteen
16) four forty-six
17) five thirty-three
18) three fifty-two
19) six seven
20) two twenty-two

UNIT 07

1.
1) is
2) is
3) am
4) is
5) am
6) are
7) is
8) are
9) is
10) are
11) is
12) are

2.
1) is
2) is
3) is
4) are
5) is
6) are
7) is
8) is
9) is
10) are
11) am
12) are

3.
1) I am a cook.
2) She is nice.
3) He is rich.
4) It is expensive.
5) They are artists.
6) She is a model. She is gorgeous.
7) He is a teacher. He is smart.
8) They are actors. They are cute.
9) We are friends. We are tall.
10) He is a man. He is nice.

4. 예)
1) I am Song Won. I am strong.
2) Derrick is a teacher. He is American. He is short.
3) Tom is a student. He is Korean. He is tall.
4) Kevin is a salesman. He is bald. He is smart.
5) Tighe is Irish. He is a recruiter. He is big.

UNIT 08

1.
1) Are
2) Is
3) Is
4) Is
5) Are
6) Are
7) Is
8) Are
9) Is
10) Are
11) Is
12) Are

2.
1) Are
2) Is
3) Are
4) Is
5) Are
6) Is
7) Is
8) Is
9) Is
10) Is
11) Are
12) Is

3

1) Is she a professor?
2) Are you a manager?
3) Is it expensive?
4) Are you serious?
5) Am I strong?
6) Is Nick a student? Is he young?
7) Is it a book? Is it difficult?
8) Are they passengers? Are they okay?
9) Is Jessica a soldier? Is she strong?
10) Is Kevin a boss? Is he rich?

4

1) Where are you?
2) Who are you?
3) What is it?
4) Where is he?
5) When is it?
6) Why is that?
7) How are they?
8) What are they?
9) Who is she?
10) Where is the bathroom/restroom/washroom?

UNIT 09

1.
1) I am not a teenager.
2) she is not a singer
3) he is not a photographer
4) they are not birds
5) it is not a computer

2.
1) I am not strong.
2) it's not expensive
3) he is not young
4) she is not okay
5) I am not hungry.

3.
1) He is not serious.
2) I am not rich.
3) We are not strangers.
4) They are not old.
5) It is not difficult.
6) She is not positive. She is negative.
7) It is not fake. It is real.
8) I am not a teenager. I am not naive.
9) They are not vegetarians. They are not fat.
10) We are not weird. We are normal.

4. 예)
1) James is not tall. He is short.
2) Kevin is not stupid. He is smart.
3) My parents are not funny. They are serious.
4) My brother is not big. He is small.
5) My sister is not strong. She is weak.
6) Tony is not a teacher. He is a student.

UNIT 10

1.
1) study
2) works
3) practice
4) learns
5) drink
6) eat
7) remembers
8) work out
9) drives
10) go
11) moves
12) run

2.
1) He drinks water.
2) He works out every day.
3) We remember you.
4) She learns fast.
5) I eat a lot.
6) I drive a bus.
7) We study hard.
8) She likes coffee.
9) They study English.
10) We go to China.
11) I live in Korea.
12) She lives in the U.S.
/She lives in the United States.
/She lives in the States.

3.
1) I study Korean because I live in Korea.
2) I study English and I work out every day.
3) I eat a lot and I drink a lot.
4) We go to China because we work in China.
5) I like coffee, so I drink coffee every day.

4.
1) I am a student, so I study every day.
2) I remember everything because I am smart.
3) She is smart, so she learns fast.
4) He is healthy because he works out.
5) I study Chinese but it is not easy.

UNIT 11

1.
1) Do
2) Does
3) Does
4) Does
5) Do
6) Do
7) Do
8) Do
9) Does

2.
1) Do you work out?
2) Do you live in England?
3) Do you like animals/cats and dogs?
   /What animals do you like?
4) At what time do you go to school?
5) Does she drink tea/green tea?

3.

1) Why do
2) When does
3) What does
4) How do
5) What does
6) Where do
7) What time do
8) How often do
9) What movie do

4.

1) How often do you work out?
2) Where do you live?
3) What kind of animals do you like?
4) At what time do you go to school?
5) How long does it take?

5. 예

1) Do you drink coffee?
Yes, I drink coffee.
2) Does she live in Korea?
Yes, she lives in Busan.
3) Do they speak English?
Sure, they speak English.
4) Does he work every day?
Yes, he works every day.
5) Do your neighbors ever say hi?
Yes, they always say hi.

UNIT 12

1.

1) I don't work
2) I don't understand
3) he doesn't care
4) I don't think so.
5) it doesn't make sense

2.

1) I don't drink wine
2) she doesn't like it
3) I don't have a car
4) she doesn't live in England.
5) they don't meet every day

3.

1) I don't speak English because I live in Korea.
2) She doesn't have money because she doesn't work.
3) He doesn't watch TV because he doesn't like it.
4) They don't work hard because they are lazy.
5) It doesn't matter because it happens a lot.

4. 예

2) My parents don't work anymore. They are retired.
3) She doesn't drink alcohol lately. She only drinks tea.
4) We don't talk to each other nowadays.
5) We aren't close friends anymore.
I don't eat meat now. I'm a vegetarian.

UNIT 13

1.
1) to
2) to
3) to
4) to
5) to
6) to
7) to
8) to
9) to

2.
1) to work out
2) to get a haircut
3) to make money
4) to watch a movie
5) to send a letter
6) to get some coffee

3.
1) to get a good job
2) to travel to Peru
3) to sell
4) to live
5) to publish them
6) to sleep

4.
1) to
2) to
3) to
4) to
5) to
6) to
7) to
8) to
9) to

5.
1) to
2) to
3) to
4) to
5) to
6) to
7) to
8) to
9) to

UNIT 14

1.
1) in
2) in
3) in
4) in
5) in
6) in
7) in
8) in
9) in

2.
1) on
2) on
3) on
4) on
5) on
6) on
7) on
8) on
9) on

3.
1) at
2) at
3) at
4) at
5) at
6) at
7) at
8) at
9) at

4.
1) on
2) in
3) on
4) on
5) in
6) in
7) at
8) in
9) on

10) at
11) in
12) on
13) in
14) in
15) on

UNIT 15

1.
1) my
2) mine
3) me
4) me
5) me
6) my
7) mine
8) my
9) me

2.
1) yours
2) you
3) your
4) you
5) you
6) yours
7) yours
8) yours
9) you

3.
1) us
2) us
3) we
4) ours
5) our
6) We
7) our
8) ours
9) our

4.
1) They
2) them
3) their
4) them
5) their
6) theirs
7) theirs
8) they
9) They

5.
1) his
2) He
3) him
4) him
5) him
6) his
7) his
8) He
9) his

6.
1) her
2) her
3) her
4) She
5) She
6) she
7) She
8) hers
9) Her

UNIT 16

1.
1) Trust
2) Ask
3) Listen up
4) confident
5) keep
6) Follow
7) Have
8) Pay attention.
9) Back off.
10) Put it down.
11) Leave
12) Be positive.

2.
1) Please come back.
2) Please put on
3) Please take off
4) Please promise
5) Please be nice
6) Please take
7) Please introduce
8) Please recommend
9) Please give

3.
1) Don't be
2) Don't be
3) Don't be
4) Don't
5) Don't
6) Don't
7) Don't
8) Don't
9) Don't be
10) Don't
11) Don't
12) Don't be

4.
1) Please don't ask
2) Please don't leave
3) Please don't be negative.
4) Please don't let her down.
5) Please don't listen
6) Please don't ruin
7) Please don't touch
8) Please don't drive
9) Please don't be too nice to him.

3.
1) often forgets.
2) often skip breakfast.
3) often misunderstand.
4) often go out at night.
5) often go there.
6) often changes her mind.
7) often argue.
8) often cries.
9) often asks many questions.

UNIT 17

1.
1) always buys things.
2) always work hard.
3) always come early.
4) Does he always make mistakes?
5) Does she always yell at you?
6) Do you always use this?
7) is always busy.
8) always smiles at me.
9) is always late.

4.
1) is sometimes annoying.
2) is sometimes useful.
3) sometimes snows.
4) sometimes smoke.
5) are sometimes wrong.
6) is sometimes weird.
7) sometimes come here.
8) sometimes watches TV.
9) sometimes happens.

2.
1) usually drinks coffee in the morning.
2) usually study at the library.
3) usually come home late.
4) Do you usually study at home?
5) Does he usually ask for a favor?
6) Does it usually snow in September?
7) usually don't study.
8) usually works from home.
9) usually doesn't snow in September.

5.
1) never drinks alcohol.
2) never cook.
3) never replies.
4) is never enough.
5) never check your email.
6) never understands.
7) is never right.
8) never listens to me.
9) never complain.

UNIT 18

1.
1) Let's
2) Let's
3) Let's
4) Let's
5) Let's be
6) Let's
7) Let's
8) Let's
9) Let's
10) Let's
11) Let's
12) Let's

2. 예
1) Let's give her a call.
2) Let's try harder.
3) Let's tell them we're on the way.
4) Let's go for dinner after the movie.
5) Let's take the train instead.
6) Let's see if she messages.

3.
1) Let's not
2) Let's not
3) Let's not be
4) Let's not
5) Let's not
6) Let's not
7) Let's not
8) Let's not
9) Let's not
10) Let's not
11) Let's not
12) Let's not

4. 예
1) Let's not rush.
2) Let's not expect too much.
3) Let's not tell her about it.
4) Let's not wait any longer.
5) Let's not fight about it.
6) Let's not turn this into a problem.

5.
1) Let me
2) Let me
3) Let me
4) Let me
5) Let her
6) Let them
7) Let us
8) Let him
9) Let me
10) Let me
11) Let me
12) Let me

6. 예
1) Let him try.
2) Would you let me help you?
3) Let me see what I can do.
4) Let her be herself.
5) My parents finally let me buy a dog.
6) He lets her use his credit card when shopping.

UNIT 19

1.
1) were
2) was
3) was
4) was
5) was
6) were
7) was
8) were
9) was
10) were
11) was
12) were

2.
1) was
2) was
3) was
4) were
5) was
6) were
7) was
8) was
9) was
10) were
11) was
12) were

3.
1) I was a coward.
2) I was a businessman.
3) He was my ex-boyfriend.
4) She was my hero.
5) You were awesome.
6) They were weird.
7) We were close.
8) I was young, and I was stupid.
   / I was young and stupid.
9) The concert was fantastic, and it was worth it.
   /The concert was fantastic and worth it.
10) She was pretty, but she was strange.
    / She was pretty, but strange.

4. 예
1) Kevin was poor.
2) Tighe was energetic.
3) Lisa was young.
4) Dylan was weak.
5) Jenny was my best friend.
6) Lisa and Jenny were very close.

UNIT 20

1.
1) Were
2) Was
3) Was
4) Was
5) Were
6) Were
7) Was
8) Were
9) Was
10) Were
11) Was
12) Were

2.
1) Were you a comedian?
2) Was she a celebrity?
3) Was he a security guard?
4) Was it a picture?
5) Were they actors?

3.
1) Was
2) Was
3) Were
4) Was
5) Were
6) Was
7) Was
8) Was
9) Was
10) Was
11) Were
12) Was

4.
1) Was it awesome?
2) Was he cute?
3) Was she adorable?
4) Was it okay?
5) Were they amazing?

5.
1) How was it?
2) Where were they?
3) Why were you there?
4) What was it?
5) When was it?
6) Who was it?

UNIT 21

1.
1) were not
2) was not
3) was not
4) was not
5) was not
6) were not
7) was not
8) were not
9) was not
10) were not
11) was not
12) were not

2.
1) I wasn't a businessman.
2) she wasn't a dancer.
3) he wasn't a designer.
4) they weren't husband and wife.
5) it wasn't a ghost.

3.
1) I wasn't tall.
2) it wasn't pricey.
3) he wasn't loud.
4) she wasn't cool.
5) I wasn't upset.

4. 예

My parents were not happy with my choices.

I was not awake during class.

You were not funny at all.

They were not so annoying.

She was not an actress.

UNIT 22

1.
1) learned a lot
2) traveled
3) talked
4) used
5) watched
6) practiced
7) loved
8) hated
9) liked
10) lived
11) rained
12) waited

2.
1) I downloaded it.
2) He dropped it.
3) We played golf.
4) My friend cooked.
5) I worked all day long.
6) I cried.
7) We returned it yesterday.
8) He called me last night.
9) We packed everything.
10) I texted her last weekend.
11) She fixed everything.
12) I finished my homework.

3.
1) I played tennis because I like to exercise.
2) He pronounced it wrong.
3) I borrowed this book from a friend of mine.
4) I charged my phone at a convenience store.
5) They helped me a lot.

4. 예)
1) I printed all of the documents.
2) She installed the program on the computer.
3) They signed up for a membership.
4) My father enjoyed the movie.
5) We searched all day long for it.

UNIT 23

1.
1) knew
2) ate/had
3) sold
4) bought
5) built
6) stole
7) did
8) heard
9) forgot
10) taught
11) told
12) paid

2.
1) I went to Canada.
2) He came.
3) She left.
4) She took a picture.
5) He found me.
6) I sent a letter.
7) They brought this.
8) She bought it.
9) I lost my phone.
10) I ate them.
11) I thought so.
12) He chose her.

3.
1) I bought a car because I needed it.
2) She took a picture and brought it here.
3) He chose her because he liked her.
4) I wrote a letter and sent it to my dad.
5) I met her, then went to the cafe to get some coffee.

4. 예)
1) I sent her a few e-mails.
2) We went to school together.
3) She made it all by herself.
4) They felt insulted.
5) My friends left earlier.

UNIT 24

1.
1) Did you
2) Did he
3) Did she
4) Did you
5) Did you guys
6) Did I
7) Did they
8) Did you
9) Did she

2.
1) Did you finish it?
2) Did she get in the taxi?
3) Did he take the subway?
4) Did you order pizza?
5) Did they get home safe?

3.
1) Why did
2) When did
3) What did
4) How did
5) Where did
6) What did
7) At what time did
8) Which country did
9) What movie did

4.
1) What did you do last Sunday?
2) At what time did you go there?
3) When did she get a haircut?
4) Where did he go yesterday?
5) How did you guys meet?

5.
1) What did you buy?
2) When/At what time did she get here?
3) Who did he bring?
4) Where did you get them?
5) What did you read?/What book did you read?

UNIT 25

1.
1) didn't answer
2) didn't know
3) didn't show up
4) didn't pay
5) didn't give up
6) didn't take a picture
7) didn't arrive
8) didn't get a haircut
9) didn't leave

2.
1) I didn't know that.
2) I didn't finish my homework.
3) he didn't go to the market.
4) she didn't come here.
5) they didn't pay.

3.
1) I didn't take a picture.
2) I didn't know.
3) I didn't meet her.
4) He didn't show up.
5) She didn't give up.

4.
1) I didn't, I was
2) she was, she didn't
3) he didn't, he wasn't
4) we didn't, was
5) I didn't, It was

UNIT 26

1.
1) for
2) for
3) for
4) for
5) for
6) for
7) for
8) for
9) for

2.
1) for recycling.
2) for playing video games.
3) for studying English.
4) for charging my phone.
5) for editing photos.

3.
1) for
2) for
3) for
4) for
5) for
6) for
7) for
8) for
9) for

4.
1) I lived in Australia for a year.
2) I waited for a few minutes.
3) He stayed here for 2 weeks.
4) She kept it for 5 months.
5) They practiced for an hour.

5.
1) for, coming
2) for, sharing
3) for, watching
4) for
5) for
6) for

UNIT 27

1.
1) am, working
2) is, exaggerating
3) are, comparing
4) is, doing
5) are, singing
6) am, doing
7) is, coming
8) is, raining
9) are, lying

2.
1) I am sleeping now.
2) I am singing at home now.
3) She is watching TV at home with a friend
4) We are working tomorrow.
5) She is coming here with her friend next week.

3.
1) are, coming
2) is, looking
3) is, getting
4) is, having
5) is, getting
6) is, barking
7) is, fixing
8) are, working
9) is, taking

4.
1) My husband is taking a picture.
2) My parents are working in Spain.
3) Tom is looking for a book at the book store.
4) John is getting on a plane at the airport.
5) Emily is having fun with her boyfriend now.

5. 예)
1) I am working from home.
2) I am meeting some friends for dinner.
3) I am visiting my grandparents in the countryside.

UNIT 28

1.
1) Are, joking
2) Is, laughing
3) Is, flirting
4) Are, having
5) Am, dreaming
6) Are, leaving
7) Is, snowing
8) Is, getting
9) Is, getting

2.
1) Are you coming?
2) Is she having fun?
3) Are you getting on the bus?
4) Is it raining now?
5) Is he leaving tomorrow?

3.
1) are, crying
2) are, doing
3) is, going
4) When are, coming
5) What movie are, watching
6) Who are, meeting
7) At what time are, meeting
8) How are, doing
9) What kind of music is, listening

4.
1) What are you doing now?
2) Where are you studying?
3) What are you studying?
4) Who are you studying with?
5) Why are you studying?

UNIT 29

1.
1) is not, concentrating
2) is not, supporting
3) am not, exaggerating
4) are not, convincing
5) is not, considering
6) am not, eating
7) are not, trying
8) are not, doing
9) is not, working

2.
1) she isn't trying hard enough.
2) they are not supporting him.
3) I'm not concentrating.
4) I'm not doing anything right now.
5) it isn't working properly.

3. 예
1) Are you kidding?
No, I'm not kidding.
2) Are you joking?
No, I'm not joking.
3) Are you laughing?
No, I'm not laughing.
4) Are you working?
No, I'm not working.
5) Are you driving?
No, I'm not driving.

4.
1) I am not working, it is Sunday.
2) he is not sleeping, he is not tired.
3) they are not coming, they are busy.
4) it is not raining, it is cloudy.
5) she is not crying, she is not happy.

5. 예)
1) What are you doing?
I'm working.
2) When is she coming?
She's coming tomorrow.
3) Why is the baby crying?
He's crying because he's tired.
4) How are they going there?
They are going by train.
5) Who is helping you with that?
My brother is helping me with that.

UNIT 30

1.
1) was, looking
2) was, fighting
3) was, yelling
4) were, taking
5) were, taking
6) were, taking
7) was, taking
8) was, taking
9) was, playing

2.
1) I was looking for my younger brother.
2) She was taking a class at school.
3) We were playing golf yesterday.
4) They were taking a walk at 2 in the morning.
5) You were taking a nap at 5 o'clock.

3.
1) I was taking a walk in the park.
2) She was taking a history class.
3) We were waiting so long for you.
4) Kevin was playing the guitar in his room.
5) Steve and Sam were playing golf together.

4.
1) I was taking a picture.
2) she was taking a walk in the park.
3) they were waiting for me.
4) I was listening to you.
5) he was taking a bath.

5. 예)
1) I was just working out.
2) Sorry. I was cooking myself some lunch.
3) I was arguing with my girlfriend.
4) I was sleeping.
5) I was taking a shower.

UNIT 31

1.
1) Were, smoking
2) Was, teaching
3) Was, snoring
4) Was, driving
5) Were, riding
6) Were, avoiding
7) Were, recording
8) Was, telling
9) Were, holding

2.
1) were, doing
2) were, going
3) were, waiting
4) Which TV show were, watching
5) What game were, playing
6) What were, making
7) What tea was, drinking
8) What book was, reading
9) What kind of music was, listening to

3.
1) What were you doing?
2) Were you waiting for me?
3) Where were you waiting?
4) What were you thinking?
5) Was he taking a nap here?

4.
1) What were you doing?
2) What were you cooking?
3) Where were you cooking?
4) Who were you cooking with?
5) Why were you cooking?

UNIT 32

1.
1) wasn't, working
2) wasn't, staring
3) wasn't, looking
4) wasn't, taking
5) weren't, talking
6) wasn't, looking
7) wasn't, waiting
8) weren't, listening
9) wasn't, enjoying

2.
1) No, I wasn't listening.
2) No, I wasn't staring at you.
3) No, he wasn't taking a nap.
4) No, she wasn't looking for you.
5) No, they weren't waiting for me.

3. 예)
1) I wasn't taking a shower. (I was watching TV.)
2) she wasn't waiting for me. (She was working.)
3) I wasn't studying at home. (I was taking a nap.)
4) he wasn't taking a nap. (He was working out.)
5) he wasn't fishing. (He was jogging.)

4. 예)
1) Were you talking to me?
No, I wasn't talking to you.
2) Was she wearing a red dress?
No, she wasn't wearing a red dress.
3) Were they waiting for us?
No, they weren't waiting for us.
4) Was your dad watching the show?
No, my dad wasn't watching the show.
5) Were the students making a lot of noise?
No, they weren't making a lot of noise.

5.
1) I wasn't buying
2) I wasn't going
3) I wasn't meeting
4) I wasn't drinking
5) I wasn't using

UNIT 33

1.
1) is going to be
2) are going to
3) are going to be
4) are going to
5) am going to be
6) is going to be
7) is going to be
8) am going to
9) is going to be

2.
1) We are going to be fine/okay/alright.
2) I am going to live here.
3) She is going to help him.
4) I am going to be a singer.
5) They are going to come.

3.
1) I am going to buy one.
2) I am going to cook.
3) we are going to come back at 10.
4) it's going to be cold at night.
5) he's going to get some sleep.

4. 예)
1) Today I am going to hang out with some friends.
2) I am going to meet them in Hongdae.
3) I am going to hang out with Tom and Blake.
4) I am going to meet them at 3 in the afternoon.
5) We are going to watch a movie and have dinner together.

5. 예)
1) Tomorrow I am going to do some shopping.
2) I am going to call my parents tomorrow.
3) I am going to buy some groceries.

UNIT 34

1.
1) Are, going to be
2) Is, going to
3) Are, going to
4) Are, going to
5) Is, going to be
6) Are, going to
7) Is, going to be
8) are, going to
9) Is, going to

2.
1) Are you going to stay here?
2) Is she going to move there?
3) Are they going to be here?
4) Are you going to be there?
5) Is your grandmother going to visit you?

3.
1) are, going to
2) are, going to
3) are, going to
4) is, going to
5) are, going to
6) are, going to
7) are, going to
8) are, going to
9) is, going to
10) are, going to

4.
1) What are you going to do tomorrow?
2) are you going to do with her?
3) are you going to leave?
4) are you going to get there?
5) are you going to stay there?

UNIT 35

1.
1) am not going to be
2) is not going to
3) are not going to
4) are not going to
5) is not going to be
6) is not going to be
7) is not going to be
8) am not going to
9) is not going to

2.
1) No, I am not going to stay here.
2) No, she is not going to leave in April.
3) No, she is not going to visit me today.
4) No, it is not going to be hot anytime soon.
5) No, they are not going to come.

3.
1) No, I am not going to come home tomorrow.
2) No, I am not going to work this weekend.
3) No, she is not going to join us.
4) No, he is not going to move out soon.
5) No, we are not going to give up.

4.
1) I am not going to do
2) I am not going to tell her
3) I am not going to start
4) I am not going to meet
5) I am not going to quit.

5. 예)
1) Are you going to do it?
No, I'm not going to do it.
2) Is she going to buy a new car?
No, she is not going to buy a new car.
3) Are they going to come?
No, they're not going to come.
4) Are we going to cook something?
No, we're not going to cook anything.
5) Are your sisters going to get married?
No, they are not going to get married.

UNIT 36

1.
1) will
2) will
3) will
4) will
5) will
6) will
7) will
8) will
9) will

2.
1) I will do it
2) I will invite
3) will give you a ride.
4) will get rid of it.
5) will figure it out.

3.
1) will be fun.
2) will show you
3) will take care of it.
4) will look it up.
5) will be, treat

4. 예)
1) I will climb the Himalaya.
2) I will get married next year.
3) I will learn to speak English.
4) I will become a millionaire.
5) I will travel around the world.
6) I will read one book a month.
7) I will work out every weekend.
8) I will buy a house for my parents.
9) I will learn to play the guitar.
10) I will stop eating junk food.

UNIT 37

1.
1) Will you
2) Will you
3) Will you
4) Will you
5) Will you
6) Will you
7) Will you
8) Will you
9) Will you

2.
1) Will you give me a ride?
2) Will you help me?
3) Will you turn off the light (for me)?
4) Will you please keep it down?
5) Will you please stop?

3.
1) I like you. Will you go out with me?
2) It's so cold. Will you turn off the A.C. (air conditioner)?
3) I miss them. When will they come?
4) It's already 3 o'clock. How long will it take?
5) He has to choose. Which one will he choose?

4.
1) What will you do today?
2) will you go to?
3) will you go with?
4) will you buy?
5) will you spend?

5.예)
1) Will you wait for me?
Of course, I will wait for you.
Take your time.
2) Will you buy me a car?
No way, I will not buy you a car.
3) What will he do with that?
I'm not sure. I guess he will try to sell it.
4) Why will you go to meet her?
She said she would treat me to dinner.
5) How will she be able to afford that?
She will probably have to save a lot of money.

UNIT 38

1.
1) will not
2) will not
3) will not
4) will not
5) will not
6) will not
7) will not
8) will not
9) will not

2.
1) No, I will not wait for you.
2) No, I will not turn off the TV.
3) No, I will not ask her out.
4) No, I will not call her again.
5) No, I will not do it again.

3.
1) No, I will not go to university.
2) No, I will not help her.
3) No, I will not forget about it.
4) No, he will not come back anytime soon.
5) No, they will not accept your suggestion.

4.
1) will not let, down
2) will not ask, out
3) will not regret
4) will not be difficult
5) will not listen

5. 예)

1) I will not fight with my brother.
2) I will not drink any more alcohol.
3) I will not be late for class.
4) I will not spend my money carelessly.
5) I will not yell at my parents.
6) I will not waste my time.

UNIT 39

1.
1) can
2) can
3) can
4) can
5) can
6) can
7) can
8) can
9) can be

2.
1) Yes, I can speak Spanish.
2) Yes, she can come to the party.
3) Yes, I can make some sandwiches.
4) Yes, I can help you.
5) No, I can open it myself.

3.
1) You can do anything.
2) He can fix everything.
3) She can feel something.
4) They can do many/a lot of/lots of things.
5) We can meet anytime.

4.
1) can teach Chinese.
2) can ice skate.
3) can make applications.
4) can make furniture.
5) can fix things.

5. 예)
1) My mother can design a dress.
2) My brother can play the drums.
3) I can dance salsa.
4) My dad can cook a decent meal.
5) My girlfriend can speak Turkish.
6) My aunt can bake cakes.

UNIT 40

1.
1) Can
2) Can
3) Can
4) Can
5) Can
6) Can
7) Can
8) Can
9) Can
10) Can
11) Can
12) Can

2.

1) Can I ask a question?
2) Can I help you?
3) Can they join the party?
4) Can we go for a walk?
5) Can I get your phone number?

3.

1) Can you
2) Can I
3) Can I
4) Can you
5) Can I

4.

1) How many languages can you speak?
2) How much can I borrow?
3) What can I do for you?
4) What kind of videos can he edit?
5) When can she finish it?

5. 예)

1) Can I buy you a drink?
2) Can we sit over there?
3) Can I call you later?
4) Can you please bring me some water?
5) Can I leave this here?
6) Can we order delivery?

UNIT
41

1.

1) can't
2) can't
3) can't
4) can't
5) can't
6) can't
7) can't
8) can't
9) can't be

2.

1) I can't trust her.
2) I can't explain it in English.
3) you can't do that.
4) we can't afford to buy a house.
5) he can't fix it.

3.

1) We can't afford (to buy) it.
2) It can't be wrong.
3) I can't accept that.
4) I can't concentrate.
5) You can't betray me like this.

4.

1) I can't speak German.
2) I can't swim
3) I can't concentrate
4) she can't afford it.
5) I can't pay

5. 예)
1) I can't do many push-ups.
2) My sister can't speak Japanese.
3) My mother can't skateboard.
4) I can't write with my left hand.
5) My brother can't lick his elbow.
6) Little kids can't reach high shelves.

UNIT 42

1.
1) want to
2) wants to
3) want to
4) wants to be
5) want to
6) want to be
7) want to
8) wants to be
9) wants to
10) want to
11) want to
12) wants to

2.
1) I want to be cool.
2) I want to be a dad.
3) I want to be a cool dad.
4) She wants to be famous.
5) He wants to ride a bike.

3. 예)
1) I want to go to Malaysia.
2) I want to meet some friends there.
3) I want to have a good time.
4) I want to meet Tun Mahadir and Siti Hasmah.
5) I want to go there next month.
6) I want to stay at an expensive hotel.
7) I want to buy a lot of souvenirs.
8) I want to eat the local cuisine.
9) I want to visit KLCC and the Central Market.
10) I want to come back in three weeks.

4. 예)
1) My dad wants to buy a building.
2) I want to build a traditional house.
3) My brother wants to live overseas.
4) My grandmother wants to visit us next year.
5) I want to be the best dancer in the world.
6) My boss wants to quit his job.

UNIT 43

1.
1) Do, want to
2) Does, want to
3) Do, want to
4) Does, want to
5) Do, want to be
6) Do, want to be
7) Does, want to
8) Do, want to be
9) Does, want to
10) Do, want to
11) Do, want to
12) Do, want to

2.
1) Do you want to buy a car?
2) Does she want to try it?
3) Do they want to live together?
4) Does he want to live in Australia?
5) Do you want to be happy?

3.
1) do, want to
2) do, want to
3) do, want to
4) does, want to
5) do, want to
6) do, want to
7) does, want to
8) do, want to
9) does, want to
10) do, want to

4.
1) Why do you want to go to Malaysia?
/Where do you want to go?
2) Why does she want to be a lawyer?
3) Who do they want to hang out with?
4) Why does he want to meet her?
5) When do they want to leave?

5. 예)
1) Do you want to go have some ice cream?
No, I want to go back home.
2) Does she want to go out with you?
No, she wants us to stay friends.
3) Do they want to collaborate with us?
Yes, they want to be a part of the project.

UNIT 44

1.
1) don't want to
2) doesn't want to be
3) don't want to
4) don't want to be
5) don't want to
6) doesn't want to
7) doesn't want to
8) doesn't want to
9) doesn't want to
10) don't want to
11) don't want to be
12) don't want to be

2.
1) No, I don't want to live with you.
2) No, she doesn't want to be with me.
3) No, I don't want to work all day long.
4) No, they don't want to work out on weekends.
5) No, I don't want to tell you everything.

3. 예)
1) Do you want to eat some pizza?
No, I don't want to eat pizza.
2) Do they want to come see us?
No, they don't want to come see us.

3) Does she want to meet your mother?
No, she doesn't want to meet my mother.
4) Do you want to take the train?
No, I don't to take the train.
5) Does he want to be the manager?
No, he doesn't want to be the manager.

4.
1) I don't want to
2) I don't want to go
3) I don't want to read
4) I don't want to do
5) I don't want to meet

5. 예)
1) I don't want to study law,
but my sister wants to.
2) I don't want to study abroad,
but my classmates want to.
3) I don't want to work for a big company,
but most people want to.

UNIT
45
1.
1) want, to
2) wants, to be
3) want, to
4) want, to
5) wants, to be
6) wants, to
7) wants, to be
8) want, to be
9) wants, to
10) want, to
11) want, to
12) wants, to be

2.
1) want, to
2) want, to
3) want, to
4) wants, to be
5) want, to
6) want, to
7) wants, to
8) want, to
9) wants, to
10) want, to
11) wants, to
12) wants, to

3.
1) wants, to
2) wants, to
3) wants, to
4) want, to
5) want, to
6) want, to
7) want, to
8) want, to
9) wants, to
10) want, to
11) want, to
12) want, to

205

4. 예)
1) I want my dad to start exercising.
2) My mom wants me to be a doctor.
3) I want him to stay for a month.
4) I want her to take me to all the most famous landmarks.
5) They want me to hang out with good people.

UNIT 46

1.
1) Do you want me to
2) Do they want him to
3) Do you want me to be
4) Does he want me to be
5) Does he want her to be
6) Does she want you to
7) Does Jenny want them to be
8) Do I want her to be
9) Do you want me to be
10) Why do you want me to

2.
1) Do you want me to stay here?
2) Do you want him to stay away from her?
3) Does he want you to take it?
4) Do they want her to take care of it?
5) Does she want them to have fun?
6) Do you want me to get better?

3.
1) Where do you want me to take you to?
2) For how long do you want them to stay here?
3) At what time does he want us to be there?
4) What do you want me to do?
5) When do they want her to come?

4. 예)
1) Why do you want me to wash your car?
2) When does she want me to come over?
3) Where do they want me to throw the party?
4) What does he want them to bring?
5) Who do you want me to call?

UNIT 47

1.
1) don't want, to be
2) don't want, to be
3) doesn't want, to be
4) don't want, to be
5) doesn't want, to be
6) don't want, to be
7) doesn't want, to be
8) doesn't want, to be

2.

1) don't want, to be
2) don't want, to be
3) don't want, to be
4) don't want, to be
5) don't want, to be
6) don't want, to be
7) doesn't want, to be
8) doesn't want, to be

3.

1) don't want, to
2) don't want, to
3) don't want, to
4) don't want, to
5) doesn't want, to
6) don't want, to
7) don't want, to
8) don't want, to

4.

1) I don't want you to
2) she doesn't want him to be
3) they don't want you to
4) he doesn't want her to be
5) I don't want them to
6) they don't want us to be
7) I don't want you to be

UNIT
48

1.

1) need to
2) need to be
3) need to
4) need to
5) need to
6) needs to
7) needs to
8) need to
9) need to be

2.

1) need to practice
2) need to save up
3) needs to work
4) needs to eat
5) need to finish

3.

1) need to stay up all night.
2) need to be business partners.
3) need to get away from everything.
4) needs to be polite.
5) need to go on a diet

4. 예)

1) I need to read more often.
2) They need to listen more carefully.
3) We need to spend more time studying.
4) She needs to be more responsible.
5) I need to stop worrying so much.
6) He needs to clean up his room.
7) My dad needs to drink less alcohol.
8) My cousin needs to find a place to stay.
9) You need to be more sincere.
10) My boss needs to be more patient.

UNIT 49

1.
1) Do, need to
2) Do, need to
3) Do, need to
4) Do, need to
5) Do, need to
6) Do, need to
7) Do, need to
8) Do, need to
9) Do, need to
10) Do, need to

2.
1) Do you need to buy it/that?
2) Do you need to take a break?
3) Do I need to tell her?
4) Do I need to get out?
5) Do we need to be polite?

3.
1) What do I need to do?
2) Who do I need to see?
3) When do you need to go to bed?
4) At what time do you need to get to the airport?
5) Where do we need to get off?

4.
1) do you need to meet her?
2) do you need to leave?
3) do we need to wait?
4) do they need to pay?
5) does she need to walk?

UNIT 50

1.
1) don't need to
2) don't need to
3) doesn't need to
4) doesn't need to be
5) don't need to
6) don't need to
7) don't need to
8) doesn't need to be

2.
1) I don't need to have a tutor.
2) we don't need to graduate from university.
3) you don't need to go all the way downstairs.
4) it doesn't need to be similar to this.
5) you don't need to have a degree.

3. 예)

1) Do you need to bring that?
No, I don't need to bring it.
2) Does she need to speak so loud?
No, she doesn't need to speak so loud.
3) Does your friend need to leave early?
No, he doesn't need to leave early.
4) Does it need to be huge?
No, it doesn't need to be huge.
5) Do you need to put eveything in boxes?
No, we don't need to put everything in boxes.

4.
1) you don't need to tell me everything.
2) you don't need to explain it again.
3) You don't need to live in the city.
4) You don't need to do it right now.
5) You don't need to tip.

5. 예)

1) You don't need to come because the meeting is over.
2) I don't need to rest because I still have a lot of energy.
3) She doesn't need to worry about that because her friend will figure it out.
4) It doesn't need to be hot because I like it cold as well.
5) We don't need to get there early because it will be starting late.

UNIT 51

1.
1) have to
2) have to
3) have to
4) have to
5) has to be
6) has to
7) has to be
8) have to
9) have to be

2.
1) have to work.
2) have to call her.
3) have to be confident.
4) have to go.
5) have to figure it out.

3. 예)

1) I have to visit my grandmother.
2) I have to leave at 9 in the morning.
3) I have to prepare for my exam.
4) I have to attend a seminar.
5) I have to graduate this year.

4. 예)

1) I have to go buy some milk.
2) I have to do my laundry.
3) I have to give my parents a call.
4) I have to iron my clothes.
5) I have to go to bed early.
6) I have to cook myself some dinner.
7) I have to tidy up my bedroom.
8) I have to take cold shower.
9) I have to take out the garbage.
10) I have to clear out my fridge.

UNIT 52

1.
1) Do, have to
2) Do, have to
3) Does, have to
4) Do, have to
5) Do, have to
6) Does, have to

2.
1) Do you have to do it?
2) Do I have to come?
3) Do we have to figure it out?
4) Do they have to be honest?
5) Do you have to get a job?

3.
1) do, have to
2) do, have to
3) do, have to
4) do, have to
5) do, have to
6) do, have to

4.
1) Why do you have to leave?
2) Where do we have to get off?
3) At what time do you have to get up?
4) What sort of jacket do I have to get?
5) What does he have to do?

UNIT 53

1.
1) doesn't have to be
2) don't have to
3) don't have to
4) don't have to
5) don't have to
6) don't have to
7) don't have to
8) doesn't have to

2.
1) you don't have to decide now.
2) I don't have to move out.
3) we don't have to do this.
4) it doesn't have to be perfect.
5) you don't have to be quiet here.

3. 예)
1) I don't have to work all day long.
2) We don't have to buy any clothes.
3) You don't have to tell me.
4) I don't have to finish it.
5) I don't have to leave.

4. 예)
1) It doesn't have to be the best.
2) We don't have to call them yet.
3) You don't have to bring any money.
4) She doesn't have to pay the entrance fee.
5) I don't have to practice that much.
6) We don't have to work so hard.
7) You don't have to be so annoyed.
8) He doesn't have to carry the boxes.
9) I don't have to be so strict.
10) She doesn't have to be a single mom.

UNIT 54

1.
1) should be
2) should be
3) should be
4) should be
5) should be
6) should be
7) should
8) should
9) should

2.
1) should be healthy.
2) should be a singer.
3) should be a chef.
4) should be smart.
5) should be successful.

3.
1) should go to bed now.
2) should make it work.
3) should be nice to my mom.
4) should get to the airport by 2:00.
5) should get away from here immediately.

4. 예)
1) I should go swimming for a while.
2) I should visit a friend at the hospital.
3) I should finish it by tonight.
4) I should meet some of my colleagues.
5) I should leave in an hour.

5. 예)
1) I think we should be more talkative.
2) I think I should give her a call.
3) I think they should clean up this mess.
4) They think we should be responsible for it.
5) We think she should come back soon.

UNIT 55

1.
1) Should
2) Should
3) Should
4) Should
5) Should
6) Should
7) Should
8) Should
9) Should

4. 예)
1) It doesn't have to be the best.
2) We don't have to call them yet.
3) You don't have to bring any money.
4) She doesn't have to pay the entrance fee.
5) I don't have to practice that much.
6) We don't have to work so hard.
7) You don't have to be so annoyed.
8) He doesn't have to carry the boxes.
9) I don't have to be so strict.
10) She doesn't have to be a single mom.

UNIT 54

1.
1) should be
2) should be
3) should be
4) should be
5) should be
6) should be
7) should
8) should
9) should

2.
1) should be healthy.
2) should be a singer.
3) should be a chef.
4) should be smart.
5) should be successful.

3.
1) should go to bed now.
2) should make it work.
3) should be nice to my mom.
4) should get to the airport by 2:00.
5) should get away from here immediately.

4.
1) I should go swimming for a while.
2) I should visit a friend at the hospital.
3) I should finish it by tonight.
4) I should meet some of my colleagues.
5) I should leave in an hour.

5. 예)
1) I think we should be more talkative.
2) I think I should give her a call.
3) I think they should clean up this mess.
4) They think we should be responsible for it.
5) We think she should come back soon.

UNIT 55

1.
1) Should
2) Should
3) Should
4) Should
5) Should
6) Should
7) Should
8) Should
9) Should

2.
1) should we meet?
2) should I do?
3) should I care?
4) should we get off?
5) should I wear a mask?
6) should I apologize?
7) should I say?
8) should I fix this?
9) should we leave?

3.
1) Why should we hire you?
2) When should I finish it?
3) When should we get off?
4) What should I do?
5) Where should we meet?

4. 예)
1) What should we bring?
You should bring an umbrella.
2) Why should I come?
You should come because it will be so much fun.
3) How should I take it?
You should pick it up with the pitchfork.
4) Where should I leave this?
You should leave it by the door.
5) When should I come over?
You should come over when I tell you to.

5. 예)
1) Do you think I should call her?
2) Do you think she should apologize?
3) Do you think we should fix it?
4) Why do you think I should care?
5) When do you think we should visit them?

UNIT
56

1.
1) shouldn't be
2) shouldn't be
3) shouldn't be
4) shouldn't be
5) shouldn't be
6) shouldn't be
7) shouldn't be
8) shouldn't be
9) shouldn't be

2.
1) shouldn't be
2) shouldn't be
3) shouldn't be
4) shouldn't be
5) shouldn't be
6) shouldn't be
7) shouldn't be
8) shouldn't be
9) shouldn't be

3.

1) shouldn't
2) shouldn't
3) shouldn't
4) shouldn't
5) shouldn't
6) shouldn't
7) shouldn't
8) shouldn't
9) shouldn't

4.

1) we shouldn't get off here.
2) you shouldn't give up now.
3) you shouldn't just do it.
4) it shouldn't be difficult.
5) we shouldn't be together.

5. 예)

1) Should I run away?
No, you shouldn't run away.
2) Should I send her some flowers?
No, you shouldn't send her some flowers.
3) Should I become a dancer?
No, you shouldn't become a dancer.
4) Should we eat it all?
No, you shouldn't eat it all.
5) Should they pack their bags?
No, they shouldn't pack their bags yet.

UNIT 57

1.

1) must be
2) must be
3) must be
4) must be
5) must be
6) must be
7) must
8) must
9) must

2.

1) must be European.
2) must be a teenager.
3) must be Allison.
4) must be a gift.
5) must be the thief.

3.

1) must be tired.
2) must be hard.
3) must be hungry.
4) must be stressed.
5) must be busy.

4.

1) must apologize
2) must call 911.
3) must finish
4) must take
5) must get

UNIT 58

1.
1) I have seen it before.
2) She has been to Spain a couple of times.
3) I have ridden a horse a few times.
4) I have tried a million times.
5) You have met him once.
6) I have heard of it before.
7) He has had surgery twice.
8) My friend has stayed here several times.

2.
1) have done it before
2) have lived, for a few years
3) has met, twice
4) have been to Italy before
5) have given a speech, a couple of times

3.
1) I have been out of the country a few times.
2) I have sung on stage
3) I have cried at school
4) I have bought clothing/clothes online
5) I have stayed up all night

4. 예)
1) I have eaten that ice cream before.
2) She has visited my hometown before.
3) We have been to a basketball game before.
4) They have done the same thing before.

5. 예)
1) I have never been to Russia before.
2) I have never read that book before.
3) She has never come to my house before.
4) We have never met each other before.

UNIT 59

1.
1) I have just cleaned up my room.
2) I have just woken up.
3) She has just changed her mind.
4) I have just received an e-mail.
5) He has just finished his homework.
6) It has just begun.
7) The package has just arrived.
8) We have just landed in Switzerland.

2.
1) He has already read the newspaper.
2) She has already sent the letter.
3) He has already made up his mind.
4) She has already passed away.
5) I have already had lunch.
6) I have already decided.
7) We have already paid for the tickets.
8) They have already shipped the samples.

3.
1) Yes, I have already locked the door.
2) No, I have just noticed it.
3) Yes, she has just left.
4) No, it has already stopped.
5) I have just sent it.

4. 예)
1) I have just called my mother.
2) She has just finished cooking.
3) We have just entered the gates.

5. 예)
1) I have already done my laundry.
2) He has already finished the project.
3) My dad has already signed the contract.

UNIT 60

1.
1) I have studied English for a long time.
2) She has traveled to many countries for 10 years.
3) We have waited for 30 minutes.
4) They have tracked your package for a week.
5) We have had a dog since 2010.
6) I have known him since high school.
7) I have tried different ways since I graduated.
8) He has driven since he was 20.

2.
1) have lived, I was little
2) have practiced for a long time
3) have been business partners for
4) has run, graduated
5) have been, since

3.
1) I have written a diary for the past 5 years.
2) I have recorded my daughter's videos since she was born.
3) He has attended job interviews since he quit his job.
4) They have been in the meeting room since they got here.
5) He has smoked cigarettes for 10 years.

4. 예)
1) I have eaten no meat for the past 2 years.
2) You have worked in that company since 2015.
3) We have lived together for a long time.
4) She has taken dancing lessons for a few months.
5) He has practiced taekwondo since he was a kid.
6) I have dreamt of being rich since I was a teenager.

UNIT 61

1.
1) He has been staring at me for 5 minutes.
2) I have been searching for him since yesterday.
3) She has been updating her résumé since she lost her job.
4) He has been begging me since he cheated on me.
5) She has been baking for 10 hours straight.
6) The kids have been crying since I got home.
7) I have been thinking about you for a long time.
8) They have been working since last night.

2.
1) have been trying
2) has been begging
3) has been changing
4) has been lying
5) has been looking for

3.
1) She has been running a restaurant for a month
2) We have been learning English for years
3) I have been using this computer
4) He has been coming here
5) I have been avoiding my ex-boyfriend

4. 예)
1) I have been taking the train every morning to go to work since I got hired.
2) I have been dating her for the past 4 months.
3) I have been feeling so frustrated after she dumped me.

UNIT 62

1.
1) would be
2) would be
3) would be
4) would be
5) would be
6) would be
7) would be
8) would be
9) would be

2.
1) would
2) would
3) would
4) would
5) would
6) would
7) would
8) would
9) would

3.
1) would
2) would be
3) would
4) would, were
5) would, did

4.
1) would call 911.
2) would get revenge.
3) would chase the bus.
4) would happen.
5) would be unhappy.

UNIT 63

1.
1) Would
2) Would
3) Would
4) Would
5) Would
6) Would
7) Would
8) Would
9) Would

2.
1) call her back?
2) keep it?
3) take it?
4) be upset?
5) grab a cab?

3.
1) would, tell
2) would, go
3) would, take
4) would, choose
5) would, know

4.
1) Would
2) Would
3) Would
4) Would
5) Would
6) Would

5.
1) turn on the light?
2) turn off the heater?
3) keep it down?
4) get rid of it?
5) consider it?

UNIT 64

1.
1) wouldn't
2) wouldn't
3) wouldn't
4) wouldn't
5) wouldn't
6) wouldn't
7) wouldn't
8) wouldn't
9) wouldn't

2.
1) wouldn't
2) wouldn't be
3) wouldn't
4) wouldn't
5) wouldn't be

3.
1) I wouldn't marry him.
2) I wouldn't take a taxi.
3) I wouldn't move to Busan.
4) I wouldn't lend it to him.
5) I wouldn't forgive her.

4.
1) I wouldn't get a puppy.
2) I wouldn't give up everything for love.
3) I wouldn't lend my friend a car.
4) I wouldn't pay $1,000 for shoes.
5) I wouldn't drink coffee instead of water.

UNIT 5

1.
1) if I were you.
2) if I were a superhero.
3) if I were a millionaire.
4) if I were free.
5) if she were here.

2.
1) if I were young.
2) if it were hard.
3) if we were lucky.
4) if it were too long.
5) if they were nice.

3.
1) if I find out.
2) if you show them.
3) if she doesn't do it.
4) if he fixes it.
5) if you don't show up.

4.
1) get, if
2) go, if
3) do, if
4) get, if
5) help, if

5. 예)
1) I would travel in time if I had a time machine.
2) I would seek help if things weren't going well.
3) I would buy a rocket if I were rich.
4) I would go to the Amazon if I were free.
5) I would be happy if I were single.

UNIT 66

1.
1) when you smile.
2) when he is here.
3) when you have time.
4) when I am free.
5) when you are sick.
6) when she works.

2.
1) when I was young.
2) when I saw him.
3) when she was a student.
4) when you were little.
5) when I was 15.
6) when I was a kid.

3.
1) when you want to hang out.
2) when I am available.
3) when he was working.
4) when I woke up.
5) when I can't sleep?

4. 예)
1) I watch TV when I am bored.
2) I was showering when it was 6 in the morning.
3) I exercise at the gym when I have time.
4) I practice English when I am free.
5) I take a taxi when I miss the last train.

UNIT 67

1.
1) There is
2) There is
3) There are
4) There is
5) There is
6) There are
7) There is
8) There are
9) There is
10) There is

2.
1) There is
2) There is
3) There is
4) There are

3.
1) There is
2) There is
3) There is
4) There is
5) There is
6) There is
7) There is
8) There is
9) There is
10) There is

4.
1) There is
2) There are
3) There are
4) There are
5) There are
6) There are
7) There is
8) There are

3.
1) There is a guy who/that
I met in Australia.
2) I am a student who/that
is looking for a job.
3) She is the one who/that
gave me a chance.
4) He is the guy who/that wrote a book.
5) I have to find someone who/that
can help me.

UNIT
68

1.
1) This is the car that I like.
2) These are the cups that we share.
3) Here is the map that shows the island.
4) This is the movie that my dad likes.
5) My mom has a new skirt that she wears every day.

2.
1) That is the book that you have to read.
2) That is the problem that I can't figure out.
3) Here is the picture that I want you to see.
4) There is something important that I have to tell you.
5) This is the jacket that I bought in France.

4.
1) She is the woman who/that I love.
2) She is the girl who/that I want to marry.
3) I have friends who/that live in Switzerland.
4) I have evidence which/that can prove it.
5) I have a cat which/that I got at a shelter.

Final Test 1

1. B	32. A	63. A	94. A
2. C	33. C	64. A	95. B
3. A	34. B	65. D	96. B
4. D	35. A	66. C	97. B
5. B	36. A	67. A	98. B
6. D	37. B	68. D	99. B
7. A	38. C	69. B	100. A
8. D	39. C	70. C	101. A
9. C	40. B	71. C	102. B
10. A	41. C	72. A	103. D
11. B	42. A	73. C	104. B
12. A	43. B	74. D	105. C
13. C	44. B	75. B	106. B
14. B	45. A	76. A	107. D
15. B	46. B	77. C	108. C
16. D	47. D	78. D	109. B
17. C	48. A	79. A	110. A
18. A	49. C	80. B	
19. B	50. D	81. D	
20. C	51. D	82. A	
21. C	52. C	83. C	
22. A	53. B	84. B	
23. B	54. A	85. A	
24. B	55. D	86. C	
25. D	56. D	87. B	
26. D	57. B	88. B	
27. A	58. A	89. B	
28. B	59. C	90. B	
29. B	60. D	91. C	
30. A	61. B	92. C	
31. D	62. A	93. A	

English Grammar for Speaking 1
(실전 영어 회화 - 기본편)

초판 1쇄	2020. 04. 10
발 행 인	송원
발 행 처	송원
주　　소	경기도 수원시 영통구 망포동 691, 104-2304
출판등록	제2016-000003호
이 메 일	rokmcsw@gmail.com
ISBN	979-11-89713-03-4

Copyright © 2020, Song Won all rights reserved.

이 책은 저작권법에 따라 무단복제와 무단전재를 금합니다.

이 책의 내용을 이용하려면 반드시 저작권자의 서면동의를 받아야 합니다.

*잘못된 책은 교환하여 드립니다.

First Published	April 10th, 2020
Written by	Song Won
Publisher	Song Won
Address	Mangpo 691, Suwon City, Gyunggi, South Korea
Publication License	제2016-000003호
Email	rokmcsw@gmail.com
ISBN	979-11-89713-03-4

Copyright © 2020, Song Won all rights reserved.